HOMESCHOOLING

the
Heart

A Study of 40 Virtues for Training a Child
in the Way He Should Go
Proverbs 22:6

KIM CORDONNIER

WESTBOW
PRESS®
A DIVISION OF THOMAS NELSON
& ZONDERVAN

As my firstfruits,
this one is for the Lord
(Who accepts earnest imperfection)

WestBow Press books may be ordered through booksellers or by contacting:

WestBow Press
A Division of Thomas Nelson & Zondervan
1663 Liberty Drive
Bloomington, IN 47403
www.westbowpress.com
1 (866) 928-1240

ISBN: 978-1-4908-8191-1 (sc)
ISBN: 978-1-4908-8192-8 (e)

Library of Congress Control Number: 2015908640

Print information available on the last page.

WestBow Press rev. date: 07/29/2015

Table of Contents

Preface

In a world where there is a great tendency to blur what is right and what is wrong, it is vital for us to thoroughly understand what *is* right. With the increase of the speed and volume of communication, it is even more necessary that we become confident in our knowledge to be able to make the hundreds of judgments necessary each day. Instilling an understanding of what is right (and hence, what is wrong) according to Scripture is essentially what *Homeschooling the Heart* intends to help you do.

This work began on a small scale, following William Bennett's *The Book of Virtues*. After a careful survey of Scripture however, I discovered that there is an even broader scope. Taking shape over many years of home-schooling my own children, the truths found in this manual have helped me to more clearly evaluate difficult situations and to ask the difficult questions. Instead of being just daunting ideals to which to live up, virtues have become valuable tools for determining what is right in God's sight. It has served my family and me well as a work-in-progress to which we have added on a regular basis— as you are encouraged to do also.

Through this study, you encounter forty virtues, what they are, how to recognize them, why they are each important, and-- perhaps most profoundly-- that they are meant to work together as a team. The goal of all virtue is to promote the greatest good, truth, and love. Isolating and idealizing some virtues while disregarding others can become a dreadful trap. We also can be easily misled by attitudes that appear to be virtuous but are really subtle distortions or not virtues at all. With so many obstacles, it is important that we arm our children and ourselves with clear understanding and confidence, which often come best from just talking and living it out together.

Ultimately, we are in desperate need of the Holy Spirit's wisdom and guidance through all our decisions. However, understanding virtue gives us the tools that our children will need to navigate through all the mixed messages they encounter in the course of a day. May you find the joys of uncovering truth on this great and noble journey together.

Introduction

Virtues are godly principles from Scripture that help us order our lives. Often they are perceived as guides to keep us on the right path, responsibilities we must try to uphold at all times, or fruit we must exhibit. While these are true, this view alone can lead to unnecessary anxiety in doing right. Virtues are also tools we have available to us to make good choices and evaluations. Like a well-equipped tool box, there are many different virtues available to accomplish a goal, each designed for a general type of job, but all for the ultimate purpose of creating something lasting. Sometimes one tool will serve the purpose better than another. A skilled worker knows what is in his tool box and which tool will work best for a particular job. But before you can become skilled, you need training and practice— a detail that should not be left to the haphazard nature of life alone.

Homeschooling the Heart is designed to help equip your children-- from a young age into adulthood-- for the purpose of becoming Christ-like. It is not meant to establish a set of rules we could use to judge ourselves or others, but rather it is meant to be a safe-haven where the principles of virtue can be explored and more fully understood. Love is always the goal— a love that most perfectly reflects the heart of our Father. Each virtue might even be considered a dimension of that love. Subsequently, when applying these principles, it is important to keep in mind that the means should never be glorified above this end. Ultimately God is the source of all virtue, so the quest itself should never be separated from having a close relationship with Him either.

You will discover that this guide is designed to be flexible, serving as an outline for you to personalize to fit you and your own family's needs. It is to be used at your discretion-- possibly as a supplemental to devotional time with read-aloud's, as the basis of individual writing assignments, or as part of a unit study. With one verse and story/chapter each school day, there is generally enough material listed under each virtue to last a month. Please fill in the margins and empty spaces with more favorite verses, hymns, books, novels, and personal stories from your family, your experiences, your imagination, or anything else you think will help your family understand principles of virtue. What you have is only the beginning.

The virtues are organized roughly according to their ease of understanding, from honesty (being accessible to the very young) to chastity (obviously, for the more mature). Most are introduced with a brief definition and its synonyms, antonyms/obstacles, imitations, and hesitations. This helps to clarify what the virtue is, what it is not, and why it may be difficult to do. A brief survey of verses and a suggested memory verse follow. The "Topic Introduction" section includes a short paragraph tailored for a younger audience with a parting discussion question. These are the types of questions you might then use to engage your children after reading a verse or literature selection. Please use any of these prompts as a catalyst to deeper discussion. Remember, the goal is understanding through critical thinking (1 Corinthians 14:20), so be sure to engage their minds with challenging queries. You may very well be surprised at the wisdom found in their answers!

The literature selections I have tried to limit to likely home-school materials available. The ones from the "Topic Introductions", for the younger ages, usually illustrate a character who either demonstrates the virtue or the lack thereof. This aids in the development of critical thinking skills and removes the sting of personal accusations. It also helps train young minds to judge situations from a Biblical world-view. The mature literature selections in the "Topic Analysis" section are full of a wide variety of themes, not only the one under which it is listed. Feel free to revise or repeat them, of course. They are there to explore a virtue, not to compartmentalize a novel. (A word of caution: please review the content before delving in, as some selections contain mature topics.)

I have chosen to refrain from including other media, such as audio dramas and movies. If you have these available, please include them where they fit. It can be a fun challenge to figure out which virtues are best illustrated by the stories in your DVD collection-- one that your children might even volunteer to do!

The "Thought Provokers" can be used as you deem appropriate. They address many issues and questions pertinent to teens and adults. They are meant to stimulate thought and discussion, opening up new possibilities of understanding and further questioning. I believe some have sound Biblical answers, while others are very vague-- a lot like life! They can get a bit deep rather quickly though, so please consider only one bullet at a time-- and add, add, add as additional issues arise.

I hope and pray that this study guide will help you and your children discover more of the great adventure and high calling we have in Christ together. Virtues are our safe-guards, challenges, and keys to true freedom. Know and use them well.

Honesty

Accurate reflection of reality

Synonyms: Truthfulness, Veracity, Uprightness

Antonyms/obstacles: dishonesty, falsehood, lying, exaggeration, flattery

Imitations: self-assertiveness, criticism

Hesitation: Opens yourself to vulnerabilities

Selected Verses

Ps. 51:6	Prov. 16:11	John 3:21	Acts 5:1-11
Prov. 11:1	Prov. 16:13	John 8:31-32	2Cor. 4:2-3
Prov. 12:17	Prov. 17:20	John 8:44	Eph. 6:14
Prov. 12:19	Prov. 19:5	John 14:6	James 3:7-8
Prov. 13:5	Prov. 24:26	John 16:13	1Peter 3:10
Prov. 13:11	Jer. 5:1-2	John 17:17	1John 1:6-8
Prov. 14:25	Zech. 8:14-17	John 18:37-38	

Memory Verse

"The LORD detests lying lips,
but he delights in men who are truthful."

Proverbs 12:22

Topic Introduction

Honesty means telling the truth--- helping others to understand the way things actually are. If we are going to work together to solve problems, we need to know how things really are. Since one person cannot see everything, honesty allows us to know better what the best course of action is. Of course, we need to be honest with God Who sees everything and knows all, too. Often, He will not go where He is not invited. Where He is invited, He wants the dark, hidden places brought into the light. Truth leads to light, for "whoever lives by the truth comes into the light" (John 3:21). That is what honesty does.

What eventually happens to most dishonest people?

Literary Examples

Literature
Pinnochio, Carlo Collodi

Short Stories
And to Think That I Saw It on Mulberry Street, Dr. Seuss

Collections

The Book of Virtues:
   "Honesty"

The Moral Compass:
   "Fish or Cat"

Aesop:
   "Boy Who Called Wolf"
   "The [Rooster] and the Fox"

McGuffey's Fourth Eclectic Reader:
   "A Chinese Story" (58)
   "The Young Witness" (74)

Thomas the Tank Engine series:
   "Bulgy" *(Oliver the Western Engine)*
   "Trucks!" *(The Little Old Engine)*

Topic Analysis

Literary Examples

"The Cactus", O. Henry

"The Count and the Wedding Guest", O. Henry

"Lost in Dress Parade", O. Henry

"Mrs. Packletide's Tiger", H. H. Munro

"The Princess and the Puma", O. Henry

The Wit and Wisdom of Abraham Lincoln, Alex Ayers

Thought Provokers

❖ It has been said that the truth may hurt but never harms; while untruth always harms. Illustrate this principle with a realistic example from your own life or one that you have heard.

❖ Honesty entails a bit more than telling the truth, for it requires trust and respect also. Cite a pair of examples to distinguish a truly honest reply from a truthful, yet opinionated one.

❖ Honesty to others often requires some discretion, for certainly there are things that other people need not know (for the sake of modesty). But if something is laid bare, we must not disguise it as something other than what it is. What is the best way to handle such an embarrassment?

❖ How do we know when to voluntarily reveal an honest truth and when to maintain a respectful silence? On the other hand, when can remaining silent be a form of dishonesty?

❖ How much of honesty is focused on the precision of fact? If a story requires a great deal of tedious detail to clarify exactly what is taking place, much can be lost in the essential message (and it can show some degree of disrespect to the listener). However, looseness of fact can result in proving ourselves to be untrustworthy. What is a good way to establish that we are capturing the essentials of a story without cluttering it with peripherals, unless further questioned?

❖ Holding someone accountable (when appropriate, though not often) is an important but difficult part of being honest. What are the difficulties in confronting someone honestly? What truths or verses might help us overcome these obstacles?

❖ It what ways do people use the phrase "Well, I'm just being honest" as a cover-up for something else? What might they really be trying to justify?

❖ Honesty, like humility, is a security-- you are standing on firm ground. Though there is sure to be opposition of one kind or another, there is no pitfall or shaky pretentiousness in it. So what could possibly be the temptation to be dishonest?

Gratitude

Gracious acknowledgment of a gift given

Synonym: Thankfulness

Antonyms/obstacles: ingratitude, demands

Imitation: thanks

Hesitation: Implies a lack of independence

Selected Verses

Lev. 22:29	Ps. 107	Rom. 14:5-6	Phil. 4:6-7
1Chr. 16:8-36	Ps. 136	1Cor. 10:30	Col. 2:7
Ps. 50:23	Mark 14:22-23	1Cor. 15:57	Col. 3:15-17
Ps. 28:6-7	Luke 17:11-19	2Cor. 2:14	Col. 4:2
Ps. 95:2	John 6:11	2Cor. 4:15	1Thes. 5:18
Ps. 100:4-5	Rom. 1:21	Eph. 5:20	Heb. 12:28-29

Memory Verse

"…since we are receiving
a kingdom that cannot be shaken,
let us be thankful…"

Hebrews 12:28

Topic Introduction

Gratitude means that you are honestly thankful for something. You see that the person gave you something of value, and you are happy to put it to good use. We can be grateful for things we can touch or things we cannot touch, like a smile or a kind word. But if we are grateful, we should make it a habit to always show our gratitude in some clear way. The only way anybody can really tell that we are grateful is if it comes out-- as a word of thanks, a hug, a look, or even turning to help someone else as a way of passing along the goodwill.

What does it feel like to give to someone who is ungrateful?

Literary Examples

Literature
Swiss Family Robinson, Johann Wyss

Hymns
"For the Beauty of the Earth",
Folliott Pierpoint
"Now Thank We All Our God",
Martin Rinckart

Short Stories
"The Elves and the Shoemaker",
Grimm brothers
"King Midas and the Golden Touch",
Greek myth
"Snow-White and Rose-Red",
Grimm brothers
"The Swineherd", Hans Christian Andersen

Collections

The Moral Compass:
   "A General Thanksgiving"
   "We Thank Thee"

Aesop:
   "Androcles and the Lion"
   "The Gardener and His Dog"
   "The Stag and the Vine"

McGuffey's Third Eclectic Reader:
   "Let It Rain" (3)

McGuffey's Fourth Eclectic Reader:
   "Harry's Riches" (25)

McGuffey's Fifth Eclectic Reader:
   "The Town Pump" (29)

Activity Idea

❖ Alphabet game-- Give thanks to God for things you cherish, beginning with each letter of the alphabet.

Topic Analysis

<u>*Literary Examples*</u>
Little Men, Louisa May Alcott
"Two Renegades", O. Henry

<u>*Thought Provokers*</u>

- ❖ Thankfulness is a perspective-adjuster, for it directs our thoughts to our blessings rather than to our burdens. It also reminds us of the Source of those blessings. What other effects might gratitude have on you? What might it have on others? List at least four.

- ❖ Is a feeling of relief a form of gratitude? Or is it a counterfeit? Relief usually comes after enduring a fearful ordeal, but it can come regardless if your part in it was noble or ignoble. Emotions, as a rule, are measures of our conditions and our place among them. So where does relief fit in?

- ❖ Paul says to "give thanks in all circumstances" (1 Thessalonians 5:18), including the bad ones. What are we affirming by being grateful in the midst of evil? How does expanding our vision via gratitude help us to persevere when we must?

- ❖ How far is reciprocity (to the extent of one's ability or resources) important in the expression of gratitude? Are you truly grateful for a significant gift or service if there is no reciprocity? Disproportional reciprocity? Only verbal thanks? The attitude of returning the favor can be manifested in the form of blessing someone else in a similar manner later on too. Are there any other objective measurements of the depth of gratitude?

- ❖ If we have been given rich gifts and tremendous promises (which, if you are in Christ, you already have been), what are we saying by *not* using them? Is it impertinent to be determined to try to do without them? What does that say about our gratitude? Our faith? Our wisdom? Our pride?

- ❖ If God is in complete control, for what should we **not** be grateful? Does being grateful mean that we *like* the situation as it stands? Does it mean we accept it? Does it mean we should resist change? In some ways, thankfulness is a confidence in the bigger picture. How can we distinguish between being grateful because of difficult circumstances or in spite of them?

- ❖ How is gratitude more than just an acknowledgment of a gift or favor, as in just saying "thank you"? Is it wrong to say "thank you" out of courtesy and not out of gratitude? In reference to thankfulness: how ought we respond when we are given "white elephant-type" gifts? What about gifts given with "strings attached"? Gifts given under obligation or begrudgingly? Ostentatious charity? Favors that do more harm than good? Flattery? Pandering? Or anything else that is meant to appear to be more than what it is?

- ❖ Oftentimes the things which appear to be curses are really blessings in disguise. Choose some thorn in your life and determine to thank God for it this week!

Obedience

Acting in response to another's instruction

Synonym: Compliance

Antonyms/obstacles: disobedience, rebellion, insubordination, debate

Imitation: heroism

Hesitations: Suppresses the will; Risk of getting lost in a trivial side-issue

Selected Verses

Gen. 22:18	Eze. 20:11	Acts 5:29-32	Heb. 11:31
Lev. 18:5	Dan. 9:4	Rom. 2:13-15	Heb. 13:17
1Sam. 15	Matt. 19:17-21	Rom. 6:16	James 1:22-25
Ps. 25:10	Matt. 28:20	Rom. 16:26	1Peter 1:14-22
Ps. 119	Luke 2:51	Eph. 6:1	1John 3:24
Prov. 10:8	Luke 11:28	Col. 3:20	
Prov. 19:16	John 14:15-24	2Thes. 3:14-15	
Jer. 7:23	John 15:10-17	2Tim. 3:2	

Memory Verse

"This is love for God:
to obey his commands.
And his commands are not burdensome..."

1 John 5:3

Topic Introduction

Obedience is prompt and complete action that follows direction given by an authority, even if you do not understand or want it yourself. Like soldiers following marching orders-- they may not know where they are going and they may not know what they are going to do once they get there-- but they trust that their commander has the final goal in mind. By marching step by step right now (or whatever other grueling job it might be), they are, to the best of their ability, aiding in the noble cause of the nation. Obedience requires trust and vision, though not often sight. And oddly enough, obedience to God is the safest thing there is, even if it is not easy.

What are often the consequences of disobedience?

Literary Examples

Literature
Charlie and the Chocolate Factory, Roald Dahl
Prince Caspian, C. S. Lewis

Picture Books
Curious George, H. A. Rey
Curious George Rides a Bike, H. A. Rey
Curious George Takes a Job, H. A. Rey
The Poky Little Puppy, Janette Lowrey
The Tale of Peter Rabbit, Beatrix Potter

Collections

The Moral Compass:
  "Henry Box Brown's Escape"

McGuffey's Third Eclectic Reader:
  "Harry and Annie" (15)

McGuffey's Fifth Eclectic Reader:
  "Capturing the Wild Horse" (80)

Thomas the Tank Engine series:
  "Down the Mine" *(Gordon the Big Engine)*
  "Off the Rails" *(Gordon the Big Engine)*
  "Percy Takes the Plunge"
      (The Eight Famous Engines)
  "Trouble in the Shed" *(Troublesome Engines)*

Additional Discussion Topics

  ❖ The Fall (Genesis 3)
  ❖ Noah (Genesis 6)
  ❖ Abraham's sacrifice of Isaac (Genesis 22:1-18)
  ❖ Jonah (Jonah 1-3)
  ❖ Partial obedience
  ❖ Promptness in obedience

Topic Analysis

Literary Examples
Paradise Lost, John Milton

Thought Provokers

- ❖ What are the consequences of not obeying God? Find a Biblical example of the effects of disobedience. List some reasons people might use for incomplete obedience. Why are the justifications we use for not following through so convincing when the consequences are comparatively so lasting?

- ❖ Submission is like obedience in that it is a yielding to another, but in submission, we usually can see clearly how it is for the best. Obedience is different in that it slices across our blind spots-- we are going where we do not understand. Which do you think is easier? Can you imagine a situation where the other would be easier?

- ❖ "To obey is better than to sacrifice" (1 Samuel 15:22). In what ways is sacrificing easier than obedience? What sorts of things do people suffer through or sacrifice to avoid obeying or to justify disobedience? What is the ultimate result of these sorts of mind games? Is there any reward from this sort of sacrifice?

- ❖ Obedience can often look deceptively like self-assertion, which caused much confusion among the Israelites in distinguishing false prophets from true ones. How can we dig deeper to more clearly identify the motivations of others? What can we do to assure *we* are truly obeying?

- ❖ Certainly we cannot and should not obey *everyone*. To whom ought we actually commit to obeying? Nor should we even obey one human always. Yet obedience should not be lightly disregarded either. So how can we disobey "in good conscience"? What should the ultimate goal be in this sort of disobedience? And how and when to apply it?

- ❖ Obedience to God often requires us to "go against the flow" of popular opinion, common sense, or even our own desires. It requires us to muster up all our strength to go and do things we are asked to do. If there are such looming un-pleasantries in obedience, how can we obey in earnest with joy?

- ❖ Ultimately, we need to act towards others in a way that will lead to the greatest love and truth. Of course, with the complexities of humanity, this is difficult to judge-- hence, the virtue study. But the dynamics are different when we are dealing with God. He already *knows* what will lead to the greatest love and truth. If we want to push towards these goals, we cannot apply reason with Him, but obedience. How might this change someone's perspective on what obedience is meant to be?

- ❖ Does true obedience necessarily need to be a free choice? What does an authority become if you have no choice but to do as they say (because the consequences are disproportional to the offense)? What do you become? Is obeying out of fear a virtue? Is it a vice?

❖ How can you distinguish between one who is following his convictions and one who is following legalistic observation of (even self-imposed) rules? Likely we should begin by respecting their choices, but what if it becomes apparent that there are harmful effects? Who are we to judge that their seemingly righteous actions are *not* obedience?

❖ Is being obedient different from just following rules? How so? In John 15, Jesus emphasizes following His commands, while He suggests elsewhere that only He can perfectly fulfill the law. How do we identify each and what should our attitude be in responding to them?

❖ What is the difference between obeying the spirit of the law and obeying the letter? How does it play out practically? What does it say about our own motivations?

Humility

Lack of thought of self

Synonym: Meekness

Antonyms/obstacles: pride, arrogance, conceit, boasting, insolence, smugness

Imitations: insecurity, indignity, self-abasement

Hesitation: Being misunderstood

Selected Verses

Judg. 8:1–3	Prov. 16:5	Matt. 5:5	James 1:21
Job 5:11	Prov. 16:18–19	Matt. 18:1–6	James 3:13
Ps. 25:9	Prov. 29:23	Luke 18:9–14	James 4:6
Ps. 147:6	Isa. 26:5–6	Rom. 12:3	James 4:10
Prov. 3:34	Isa. 57:15	Rom. 12:10	James 4:13–16
Prov. 11:2	Jer. 9:23–24	Rom. 12:16	1Peter 4:11
Prov. 13:10	Jer. 45:5	1Cor. 1:28–29	1Peter 5:5–6
Prov. 15:25	Eze. 21:26	1Cor. 5:6–8	
Prov. 15:33	Dan. 4:28–37	Gal. 6:3–5	

Memory Verses

"Do nothing out of selfish ambition or vain conceit,
but in humility consider others better than yourselves."

Philippians 2:3

"'He must become greater; I must become less.'"

John 3:30

Topic Introduction

Humility means that you do not think about making yourself important but are more interested in using what you have to do the most good for everybody. If we are not going to worry about what other people think of us, then we must be confident in what God thinks of us. We are each incredibly valuable in God's eyes. You are special just the way He made you, and He can take care of shaping you into the hero that will change your corner of the world. You do not have to worry about that (except to keep obeying). If you are His child, you are already important. So humility is putting the climb aside to be available for doing the truly great things, even if they are not noticeable.

What are the dangers of being proud?

Literary Examples

Short Stories

"The Big Brag", *Yertle the Turtle*
            and Other Stories, Dr. Seuss
"Brave Little Tailor", Grimm brothers
"The Gingerbread Man", traditional tale
Tikki Tikki Tembo, Arlene Mosel
"Yertle the Turtle", *Yertle the Turtle*
            and Other Stories, Dr. Seuss

Hymn

"When I Survey the Wondrous Cross",
                                    Isaac Watts

Collections

The Moral Compass:
    "Arachne"
    "The Gold Bread"
    "Man Enough for the Job"

Aesop:
    "The Farthing Rushlight"
    "The Fighting [Roosters] and the Eagle"
    "The Fir Tree and the Bramble"
    "The Frog and the Ox"
    "The Monkey and the Camel"

McGuffey's Third Eclectic Reader:
    "The Clock and the Sundial" (28)

McGuffey's Fifth Eclectic Reader:
    "The Will" (54)

Thomas the Tank Engine series:
    "Buzz, Buzz" *(Main Line Engines)*
    "Dirty Objects" *(Toby the Tram Engine)*
    "Henry and the Elephant"
                    (Troublesome Engines)
    "James and the Express"
                    (James the Red Engine)
    "Mike's Whistle" *(Small Railway Engines)*
    "Percy and the Signal"
                    (Percy the Small Engine)
    "Resource and Sagacity"
                    (Oliver the Western Engine)
    "Thomas Comes to Breakfast"
                    (Branch Line Engines)
    "Wrong Road" *(Main Line Engines)*

- ❖ Tower of Babel (Genesis 11:1-9)
- ❖ Being a good sport

Activity Idea

- ❖ "War" card game variation with low cards beating high cards

Topic Analysis

Literary Examples

Johnny Tremain, Esther Forbes
Pygmalion, George Bernard Shaw
"The Sphinx Apple", O. Henry
"The Storyteller", H. H. Munro

Thought Provokers

- ❖ Often humility is thought of as being a self-debasing attitude ("Oh, I'm no good at that." or "I'm so unworthy, so this is what I try to do about it..."). How can this view of humility lead directly to pride? Is this the sort of "false humility" referred to in Colossians 2:18? How can it be recognized as such? What would be a good response to someone who advocates this attitude?
- ❖ Sometimes "pride" has a positive connotation. Is there such a thing as "good pride" or is it just a misnomer for a different virtue?
- ❖ Meekness is often misjudged as weakness. What *is* the difference? Though you may not be able to convince others, how can you strive for one without giving into the other?
- ❖ With humility come many virtues, for then you have access to those of others. Find an example of this. Are there other virtues that work similarly?
- ❖ What is the difference between dignity and pride? What are their distinguishing characteristics? While we are called to uphold human dignity, we are not to encourage self-centered pride. So how do we identify each so that we know how to respond to it?
- ❖ While being broken is dreadfully unpleasant, there is a good deal of benefit to being at the bottom. There is no more pretense, no real risk in boldly stepping out, and a clearer vision of what is really important. Find three more advantages.
- ❖ Often making excuses for ourselves (however legitimate) is a form of pride, in that we intend to justify ourselves or our actions. Simple courtesy can usually cover the situation far better than tedious excuses can. When would brief explanations be appropriate though? When does an explanation cross the line and become an excuse?

❖ Receiving praise can create a dilemma, in that encouragement is indeed sweet but we must also be wary of it inflating into pride. What humble attitude should we have in this situation? What then would be a good response to someone's praise (assuming it is not flattery)?

❖ As the topic introduction paragraph suggests, is pride really just a sham to appear-- and hence feel-- important? What are some methods that people employ to build their own sense of importance, and hence, security? How strongly do they hold to these identities? Do they work?

❖ A root of pride has many distinguishing fruits, such as comfortable settled-ness and self-confidence. List some of these characteristics. Then list their opposites. What does this say about humility?

Patience

Waiting when it gets difficult to wait;
Slowness to anger or anxiety

Synonym: Forbearance

Antonyms/obstacles: impatience, haste, anxiousness, frustration, rage, insecurity, quick-temper

Imitation: tolerance

Hesitation: Wasted time

Selected Verses

Gen. 8:1-15	Prov. 14:17	Amos 5:13	1Thes. 5:14
Gen. 40:23-41:14	Prov. 14:29	Hab. 2:3	Heb. 6:12-15
1Sam. 13:5-14	Prov. 15:18	Luke 21:19	Heb. 10:35-38
Ps. 37:7-13	Prov. 16:32	Rom. 8:25	James 5:7-11
Ps. 40:1-3	Isa. 30:18	Rom. 12:12	2Peter 3:15
Ps. 130:5-6	Isa. 64:4	1Cor. 13:4	

Memory Verse

"Wait for the LORD;
be strong and take heart
and wait for the LORD."

Psalm 27:14

Topic Introduction

Patience is all about waiting. In waiting, it seems we do nothing and see nothing, so it feels like patience is absolutely nothing. What good can come from nothing? So it is easy to get anxious or angry and do *something*-- but then that is not patience. But God's ways are mysterious, His timing is perfect, and He often does incredibly more in our waiting than in our working. Maybe He does this because He wants to show us that He is the One doing the working while we are waiting— so that He can take all the credit for the good results, as of course He deserves. Take heart, God created a whole universe out of nothing, so patience *is* rich ground for a fruitful harvest. Just hang in there!

What usually happens when someone acts out of impatience?

Literary Examples

Literature
Farmer Boy, Laura Ingalls Wilder
Ribsy, Beverly Cleary
Through the Looking Glass, Lewis Carroll

Collections

McGuffey's Fourth Eclectic Reader:
    "Strawberries" (24)

McGuffey's Fifth Eclectic Reader:
    "Control Your Temper" (66)

Thomas the Tank Engine series:
    "Better Late than Never"
        (*More About Thomas the Tank Engine*)
    "Thomas' Train" (*Thomas the Tank Engine*)

Additional Discussion Topics

- ❖ Abraham for a son (Genesis 15-21)
- ❖ Joseph in prison (Genesis 39-41)
- ❖ Trying "too hard"

Topic Analysis

Literary Examples
The Miracle Worker, William Gibson
Robinson Crusoe, Daniel Defoe

Thought Provokers

- ❖ Why might patience be considered a sort of diligence? How might patience be a fruit of peace?
- ❖ Is it possible to be *too* patient with another person? Is "losing your patience" necessarily always a bad thing? How so? Find a Biblical example of people exasperating God's patience. Does this set us an example or not?
- ❖ It seems that while virtues must be carefully nurtured, vices are natural and even contagious. Give an example of how impatience can be contagious.
- ❖ How is tolerance different from patience? How can we be intolerant of wrong belief or behavior and still be patient?
- ❖ God can be very slow by our terms. If He gives us some insight, we often have this great expectancy that the results (and what we believe are their implications) are imminent. Of course, this is sometimes true. But sometimes in our zeal to fulfill the vision (or even just understand it), we become hasty. Sarah's idea to raise an heir through Hagar is an example of this (though humanly speaking, she was technically true to the promise). The results of her subtle disobedience and impatience are still felt today. Why are the consequences of this kind of sin so far reaching?
- ❖ We must have a good understanding of what God is asking from us and remain in good communication with Him, because patience can be used as a mask for many vices. Describe how patience might be used as an excuse for indifference, disobedience, unbelief, or laziness.
- ❖ "A watched pot never boils" is a famous proverb about patience. What might it suggest we must do if our duty (chosen or forced) is to be patient? Practically, what does this look like? Even though internally we may be full of uncertainty and weariness, noble external distractions are invaluable. Name someone who was patient in affliction and remained so more easily by keeping busy doing good.

Courage

Fighting for an intangible good despite a tangible threat

Synonyms: Bravery, Valor

Antonyms/obstacles: cowardice, panic

Imitation: pluck

Hesitation: Failure with needless sacrifice

Selected Verses

Deut. 31:6–8	Ps. 107:26–29	Matt. 14:27–33	2Cor. 4:16–18
Josh. 1:1–9	Ps. 138:3	Luke 12:4–7	Eph. 6:10–12
Josh. 10:25	Prov. 28:1	Acts 4:1–13	Phil. 1:20
1Chr. 22:13	Isa. 35:4	1Cor. 1:7–9	Heb. 3:6
Ps. 27:13–14	Dan. 3:17–18	1Cor. 16:13–14	1Peter 3:15–16

Memory Verse

"'In this world you will have trouble.
But take heart!
I have overcome the world.'"

John 16:33

Topic Introduction

Courage is doing or saying something to fight for good, even when-- or especially when-- it might hurt. Courage does not mean that we are not afraid, but that we are willing to stand up for something even though we are afraid. Sometimes speaking up for right is more important than feeling safe. And it can be inspiring-- when we help others stand up for what is right and true, too. But courage is not just for the soldier or missionary-- it is for everyone. God has called each of His children to shine for Him, and shining is brave when so many others say that darkness is better.

What are the emotions of someone who has made the cowardly choice?

Literary/ Musical Examples

<u>Short Stories</u>
"Issun Boshi: One-Inch Boy",

Japanese folktale
The Matchlock Gun, Walter D. Edmonds

<u>Musical Pieces</u>
"A Mighty Fortress is Our God",

Martin Luther
Peter and the Wolf, Sergei Prokofiev

Collections

The Book of Virtues:
   "Courage"

The Moral Compass:
   "The Chevalier D'Assas"
   "The Little Girl Who Dared"
   "Northwest Passage"

McGuffey's Third Eclectic Reader:
   "Courage and Cowardice" (30)

McGuffey's Fifth Eclectic Reader:
   "The Crazy Engineer" (69)

Additional Discussion Topics

❖ Spiritual Armor (Ephesians 6:14-18)
❖ Daniel and the Lion's Den (Daniel 6)
❖ Fiery Furnace (Daniel 3)
❖ David and Goliath (1 Samuel 17)

"An Afternoon Miracle", O. Henry
The Red Badge of Courage, Stephen Crane
The Lord of the Rings, J. R. R. Tolkien
Sea Wolf, Jack London

Thought Provokers

- ❖ Courage nearly invariably involves a fight. It might be against the elements, against others, against a dangerous philosophy, or within your own mind. The difficult dilemma often comes in weighing the costs. Make a list of the things that are most important and worth protecting with a battle. Do you believe in them enough to put up a fight, if necessary?
- ❖ When is a daring deed fool-hardiness, and when is it courage?
- ❖ Sometimes we might act courageously out of a sense of the heroic or romantic. Is this necessarily wrong? Is it just another form of fool-hardiness? What is a better motivation for courage?
- ❖ Being aware of our own vulnerabilities is a first step towards courage. What are the following steps?
- ❖ Courage is one of the few virtues that we cannot determinedly do very well; as it is more something that we must be prepared to do as the occasion arises. What might be the effects of someone setting out with the intent of being courageous? How then can we build courage?
- ❖ Often cowards talk where the courageous act. How can talking become a pitfall where action is required? What is a good response to someone who appears to be doing this?
- ❖ Courage requires risk-- entering into the uncertain to accomplish something better. Sometimes assessing risk can aid in acting courageously, but sometimes it only hinders or halts it entirely. When is weighing the risks wise and when is it counter-productive?
- ❖ Courage is what it takes to overcome some real or potential threat. List some of these specific threats that you have observed in history or your own experience. (They might include something we could lose-- tangible or intangible, enemies that we could make, or something else that we might stir up that has an uncertain outcome.) What might be the greater good in the end though?
- ❖ Often courage is a catalyst to great things. Where have you seen someone's courage inspiring others to stand up for what is right also? What major events in history have begun with great courage from a group or individual?
- ❖ Give an example of a time you (or someone else) acted courageously. Was the fight as difficult as it might have been? Was there any degree of success in standing up for right? Often our fears are more lurking than the actualities; though we must also be prepared for the worst. What has been your experience with this, and how has it affected your willingness to act courageously again?

Faith

*Believing another's trustworthy testimony despite reasons not to;
God-confidence*

Synonym: Trust

Antonyms/obstacles: doubt, worry, distrust, mistrust, incredulity, skepticism, fanaticism, self-reliance

Imitations: religious activity, blind faith, mere assent, presupposition

Hesitation: Risk in leaving the security of human reasoning or alternate plans

Selected Verses

Ps. 4:3	Isa. 30:15	Luke 7:1–10	1Thes. 5:8
Ps. 9:9–10	Isa. 33:16–21	John 3:15–18	Heb. 11
Ps. 18:1–3	Isa. 55:8–9	Acts 16:31	James 1:6–8
Ps. 40	Matt. 6:8	Rom. 4:18–24	James 2:14–26
Ps. 73:23–26	Matt. 6:25–27	Rom. 5:1–2	1Jn 5:1–10
Ps. 121	Matt. 14:22–33	Rom. 14:22–23	
Prov. 3:5–6	Mark 5:25–34	Gal. 3:5–9	
Isa. 26:4	Mark 11:22–24	Eph. 6:16	

Memory Verse

"Now faith is being sure of what we hope for
and certain of what we do not see."

Hebrews 11:1

Topic Introduction

The Bible says, "Faith is being sure of what we hope for and certain of what we do not see" (Hebrews 11:1). It is a little like having a secret pair of eyes that can see what God has done, what God is like, and what God has promised all wrapped up in the truth that He loves us like crazy. What we see and understand is often very different from what God has to say, so faith means we choose to err on the side of God's Word rather than on our own senses. Even though there are many choices, faith thoughtfully chooses the one with the strongest Supporter. We can also have faith in other people, though to a much lesser degree. It means that we trust what they do and why they do it, even if we do not understand the methods they use.

How does a person who has no faith in God find a reason to live?

Literary Examples

Literature
The Lion, the Witch, and the Wardrobe,
C. S. Lewis

Short Story
The Tale of Ginger and Pickles, Beatrix Potter

Hymns
"He's Got the Whole World in His Hands",
traditional
"I Need Thee Every Hour", Annie S. Hawks
"Leaning on the Everlasting Arms",
Elisha Hoffman
"The Old Rugged Cross", George Bernard
"'Tis So Sweet to Trust in Jesus",
Louisa M. R. Stead

Collections

The Book of Virtues:
"Faith"

McGuffey's Fourth Eclectic Reader:
"The Tempest" (45)

McGuffey's Fifth Eclectic Reader:
"William Tell" (67-68)

Thomas the Tank Engine series:
"Mountain Engine" *(Mountain Engines)*

Additional Discussion Topics

- ❖ F.A.I.T.H. acronym (**F**orsaking **A**ll, **I T**rust **H**im)
- ❖ Faith versus religion

Topic Analysis

Literary Examples

Brothers Karamozov, Fyodor Dostoyevsky
"The Green Door", O. Henry
Hinds Feet on High Places, Hannah Hurnard
Pilgrim's Progress, John Bunyan

Thought Provokers

- ❖ What characterizes "religion"? How is it different from "faith" as depicted in Scripture? Make a table which highlights these differences. (Include topics such as "Motivation for doing good", "Evidence of zeal", and "What freedom it offers")

- ❖ All people have some sort of faith. What are some examples of things in which they might put their faith? What are the fruits of these faiths?

- ❖ There needs to be a certain degree of reckless trust in faith but not foolish recklessness. How can you tell the difference? Should we look for reassurances once we have stepped out in faith or is that really just a form of doubting?

- ❖ What is the difference between faith and superstition? Where is this line particularly fuzzy? Similarly, how is having a faith in "faith" (the power of visualization with expectation) or faith in principles (even if godly) distinct from having faith in Christ?

- ❖ Much of Jesus' dealings with the crowds revealed his power and goodness, but He also had a strong underlying focus on dispelling expectations of what He should be or do (find some of these incidences). How is dissolving expectations a key to faith?

- ❖ How is trust different (and much more work) than a fatalistic attitude (i.e., "que sera sera")? Explain.

- ❖ Compare faith as "God-confidence" to building and maintaining other types of confidences.

- ❖ Does faith stand opposed to common sense? Surely if you rely solely on common sense, or even solely on blind faith, you become disconnected from reality. Either way, you can easily (and stubbornly) be believing (and suffering) something that is neither "working" nor blessed. What is a good principle for knowing when to rest on which?

- ❖ When we truly step out in faith, it is often proved right in reality, and then we are much encouraged in our faith. Though difficult to start, this can be a beautiful cycle. But what if the realities do not seem to be manifesting? How can you know if it is just a test and you should persevere or if you have really gone astray and should restart?

- ❖ Is doubt always an obstacle to faith or is it sometimes an aspect of faith? If "faith… is being certain of what we do not see" (Hebrews 11:1), then what is being certain of what we *do* see? Is doubt the necessary "not seeing"? Yet too much doubt can throw us completely out of faith also. So how much uncertainty/doubt is healthy and necessary, and how much is harmful?

- ❖ Many times we say that we believe something strongly, but when push comes to shove, we fail to uphold it. How is belief transformed into faith? Describe an example of this.

23

❖ Being presumptuous is often a characteristic of being thoughtless, selfish, and/or prideful. Yet at the same time, stolidly avoiding being presumptuous can also be a violation of integrity, humility, and honesty. Little children are perhaps the most presumptuous of all people, yet we are to be like little children to our Heavenly Father! (Matthew 18:3) What *should* our attitude be towards another (or God) when we need help from him? Is it possible to be presumptuous in asking for a gift when it has already been promised to you (directly or indirectly)? How does a trusting attitude look different from a presumptuous one?

Diligence

Focused effort for a greater good-- despite internal obstacles

Synonyms: Discipline, Persistence, Steadfastness, Resolution

Antonyms/obstacles: distractions, shortsightedness, idleness

Imitation: stubbornness

Hesitation: Wasted energy

Selected Verses

Gen. 3:17-19	Prov. 6:6-8	Isa. 26:3	Col. 1:22-23
Gen. 18:16-33	Prov. 10:4-5	Rom. 2:7	1Thes. 4:11-12
2Kings 5:1-14	Prov. 13:4	1Cor. 9:24-27	2Thes. 3:6-10
Neh. 4:6	Prov. 14:23	Gal. 6:9	1Tim. 4:15
Ps. 119:4-6	Prov. 21:5	Eph. 4:28	Heb. 12:1
Prov. 4:25-27	Ecc. 10:10	Eph. 6:10-13	1Peter 5:8-10

Memory Verse

"Therefore, my dear brothers, stand firm.
Let nothing move you.
Always give yourselves fully to the work of the Lord,
because you know that your labor in the Lord is not in vain."

1 Corinthians 15:58

Topic Introduction

Diligence means that you keep working for something that is important even when you would rather give it up. It means work-- often long, hard, tedious work. But usually our diligence has an end and a finished product, a sweet reward that can even outlast our lifetime. If we choose to keep at it, we can begin to see the difference we can make in our world-- and it gets easier! Every object of value took diligence and skill to create (and even skill does not come without diligence). So be diligent in the little things, and see your effort multiply into big things with God.

What happens to people who cannot keep a job because they are not diligent?

Literary Examples

Picture Books
Are You My Mother?, P. D. Eastmann
Ox-Cart Man, Donald Hall

Poem
"Itsy, Bitsy Spider", nursery rhyme

Collections

Book of Virtues:
  "Work"

The Moral Compass:
  "The Man Who Moved the Earth"
  "Rip Van Winkle"
  "The Sculptor and the Sistine Chapel"
  "Why the Water in Rivers is Never Still"

Aesop:
  "The Farmer and His Sons"
  "The Hare and the Hound"
  "The Tortoise and the Hare"
  "The Wind and the Sun"

McGuffey's Third Eclectic Reader:
  "Persevere" (59)

McGuffey's Fourth Eclectic Reader:
  "Where There's a Will There's a
                                    Way" (12)
  "Consequences of Idleness" (39)
  "Advantages of Industry" (40)
  "Hugh Idle and Mr. Toil" (79-80)

McGuffey's Fifth Eclectic Reader:
  "Work" (8)
  "The Discontented Pendulum" (33)
  "The Village Blacksmith" (46)
  "Sowing and Reaping" (81)

Activity Idea

❖ Put together a 1000 piece puzzle

Literary Examples

The Old Man and the Sea, Ernest Hemingway

Thought Provokers

- ❖ When is determination diligence and when is it stubbornness? How do you know when you have crossed the line from one to the other?
- ❖ How is perseverance different from diligence?
- ❖ What are some common obstacles to diligence today? How might these be different from those a century ago?
- ❖ Diligence is one of the few virtues with tangible benefits. There is satisfaction in seeing a job well-done. It is sometimes also motivated by necessity. So what would be the best way to teach its importance to an unmotivated person?
- ❖ Most people who have accomplished great things have done so through their dedication and diligent efforts. Name someone whom you admire for what he has accomplished and speculate on the obstacles he had to overcome in his own mind to achieve that goal.
- ❖ Most of us have a sort of "selective diligence," where we can be extremely dogged at beating a sports goal or video game level but are much more prone to complain about daily chores, tedious work, or even prayer. How can we redirect this "selective" motivation to encourage ourselves to be more diligent in the things that really matter? What keeps us more absorbed with the trivial than with the vital?
- ❖ Diligence requires vision to trudge through the difficulties in our own minds. What is something that you believe is your calling or vision? In what ways have you been or might you be tempted to give up the cause?

Modesty

Care with the use and display of the body and other delicate matters

Synonyms: Discretion, Decency

Antonyms/obstacles: immodesty, obscenity, vanity, shamelessness, flirting, lewdness, indiscretion

Imitation: self-consciousness

Hesitation: Risk of being ignored

Selected Verses

Gen. 3:7, 21	Est. 2:12-15	Mark 5:1-15	Eph. 5:4
Gen. 9:20-23	Prov. 11:22	Rom. 12:2	1Thes. 4:4
Ex. 34:29-35	SOS 2:7	Rom. 13:13-14	1Tim. 2:9-10
Lev. 19:28	Isa. 3:16-24	1Cor. 6:19-20	1Peter 3:1-6
Deut. 22:5	Eze. 16:7-14	1Cor. 11:4-15	
2Sam.14:25-18:9	Matt. 18:9	1Cor. 12:22-26	

Memory Verse

"…you were bought at a price.
Therefore honor God with your body."

1 Corinthians 6:20

Topic Introduction

Modesty means that we avoid drawing unnecessary attention to ourselves or any other topic that should be addressed with care. Often this applies to what we wear-- in that we should not generally dress in a flashy manner or with clothing that does not adequately cover our bodies. It can also apply to our speech and gestures, where we should not say or do things that imply vulgarity. Other ways of communicating too should be modest-- writing, art, dance, touch, even the display of what you own. But modesty is ultimately for the sake of others, so that we do not cause them discomfort or tempt them to have unwholesome thoughts.

Would dressing immodestly help you to be liked for who you really are?

Literary Examples

Literature
Thee, Hannah!, Marguerite de Angeli

Short Stories
"The Emperor's New Clothes",
　　　　　　　　Hans Christian Andersen
"The King's Flower", Mitsumasa Anno
"Prince Hyacinth and the Dear Little
　　　　Princess", Madame Leprince de Beaumont

Collections

The Moral Compass:
　"How Hippo was Humbled"

Aesop:
　"The Bald Knight"

McGuffey's Third Eclectic Reader:
　"The Little Bird's Song" (14)

Thomas the Tank Engine series:
　"Gordon's Whistle"
　　　　　　(Henry the Green Engine)

Additional Discussion Topics

❖ Good grooming habits
❖ Appropriate topics of discussion in various situations

Activity Idea

❖ "Redress" immodestly dressed people in advertisements with markers

Topic Analysis

Literary and Dramatic Examples
The Great Gatsby, F. Scott Fitzgerald
La Sonnambula, Vincenzo Bellini (an opera)
"The Mouse", H. H. Munro
"The Necklace", Guy de Maupassant

Thought Provokers

- ❖ "Modesty" is often used interchangeably with "humility". Why? Why should it be considered separate though?

- ❖ How might self-consciousness be mistaken for modesty? How can they be distinguished?

- ❖ It is conceivable that modesty can be taken to an extreme. We certainly should try to look our best without becoming immodest. What are some good principles to apply for discerning how to dress?

- ❖ Modesty also applies to our motions, our gestures, and our facial expressions. One of the best ways to judge if something is inappropriate is to think if someone in particular (like your grandmother) were with you, would she be embarrassed by you. Who do you respect that might serve as this imaginary guide? What is a better alternative to our immodest habits?

- ❖ Is most immodesty really just an appeal for attention? Support your opinion.

- ❖ If it is necessary to be the object of attention-- whether as a teacher, speaker, entertainer, or in any other visible position-- how can we maintain a modest attitude? Actually, Jesus calls us to shine as lights in the darkness (Matthew 5:14), so how would this *not* be vanity? What makes the difference obvious to observers?

- ❖ Immodesty is often excused as an art form. How does reducing someone (even an imaginary character) to an art subject interfere with human dignity? Or does it truly *not* serve as a great distraction in an immodest "work of art"?

- ❖ Modesty also applies to topics of discussion. Certainly there are some subjects which should not be discussed with a general audience. However, within the proper context and ultimately for the protection of virtue, these subjects *should* be addressed and brought into the light. What is the best method for addressing these "unmentionables"? Conversely, what kinds of topics should never be discussed, at least not in detail? (Ephesians 5:12)

- ❖ Modesty is something we must strive to defend in others also. Generally we should not even discuss immodest situations, if only out of respect for others. But there are times when shameful behavior necessarily must be exposed for the greater good of another-- though even this should be done delicately. So how far should we strive to cover-up another's shame and when do we need to step up to expose it? And then how?

Generosity

Giving beyond expectation or merit, without considering the cost

Synonym: Grace

Antonyms/obstacles: over-cautiousness, stealing, stinginess

Imitations: indulgence, cheap generosity

Hesitation: Limits your resources

Selected Verses

Ex. 35:4–36:7	Prov. 18:16	Matt. 5:38–42	Acts 4:32–37
Deut. 15:7–11	Prov. 19:6	Matt. 6:1–4	Acts 20:35
1Chr. 29:1–9	Prov. 21:26	Matt. 7:9–12	Rom. 12:6–8
Ps. 37:25–26	Prov. 22:9	Matt. 20:1–16	2Cor. 8:2–7
Ps. 112:5	Prov. 28:22	Mark 12:41–44	2Cor. 9:6–11
Prov. 11:24–26	Ecc. 11:2	Luke 12:13–21	1Tim. 6:17–19

Memory Verses

"'Freely you have received, freely give.'"

Matthew 10:8b

"'Give, and it will be given to you.
A good measure, pressed down,
shaken together and running over,
will be poured into your lap.
For the measure you use,
it will be measured to you.'"

Luke 6:38

Topic Introduction

Generosity means giving far more than you were expected to give. It means that you are willing to give up some of what you want for yourself to really help someone else. Generosity does not always have to be money, either-- it can be sharing anything at all that you value. (What are some things that people value which might be offered as a generous gift to another?) But to give generously, you have to want to give it yourself, and it is even better if it is your own idea! What did God give you generously, that was His own idea? How would you like to pass it on?

How have you seen that God *delights* to give even more to people who give generously?

Literary Examples

Literature
Eight Cousins, Louisa May Alcott

Short Stories
"A Christmas Carol", Charles Dickens
Stone Soup, folktale

Hymns
"Amazing Grace", John Newton
"And Can It Be?", Charles Wesley

Collections

The Book of Virtues:
  "The Selfish Giant"

The Moral Compass:
  "The Unfruitful Tree"

Aesop:
  "The Dog in the Manger"
  "The Miser"

McGuffey's Third Eclectic Reader:
  "The Widow and the Merchant" (18)

McGuffey's Fourth Eclectic Reader:
  "Emulation" (48)

McGuffey's Fifth Eclectic Reader:
  "The Generous Russian Peasant" (43)

Additional Discussion Topics

❖ G.R.A.C.E. acronym (**G**od's **R**iches **A**t **C**hrist's **E**xpense)
❖ Getting married

Topic Analysis

Thought Provokers

❖ The value of money (or talents or experience) lies not in what it can accomplish, but in what it can do when given away. What are some intangible gifts given with generous, tangible ones?

❖ Generosity implies a whole-hearted support of a people or cause. How far must we judge the soundness of the investment before giving abundantly?

❖ How do we know when we have crossed over from generosity into un-beneficial indulgence? Must it be so carefully administered in order that it does not become a continuous obligation or a minimal expectation, devoid of joy? Are most acts of generosity best understood as a one-time gift then?

❖ Is there ever a time when we should be generous, even against our desire or will? Whose will or what obligation supersedes our own in terms of generosity? What if others will suffer real harm if we do *not* give? If we must give, ought we not do it with utmost grace and effort as if we were serving the Lord? Support your opinion.

❖ Should you be generous to someone who will not appreciate the sacrifice (either by taking advantage of you or by not valuing it)? Should you give to someone-- whom you know from experience or reputation-- who has no intention of ever returning the favor, even if they could? Illustrate with examples.

❖ Acts of generosity are often met with the charge of being unfair. For example, see the parable of the Workers in the Vineyard (Matthew 20:1-16). What are the underlying assumptions to this mistake, and how are they best dispelled?

❖ While we should try not to become dependent on the generosity of others (though at times, it can come as a huge blessing), we do need to rely and depend on the grace of God continually. Compare and contrast the nature of these two great gifts/givers.

❖ Grace is sort of a super-saturated form of generosity that completely outstrips any possible merit. But generally grace should not be bestowed on a person until they are capable of understanding what is happening-- the huge disparity between what is deserved and what is received. Illustrate this principle with an example.

❖ If grace is a gift that follows from honestly and humbly facing the reality of our own spiritual condition-- ultimately leading to freedom-- what does the other path(s) look like? Make a diagram illustrating a life with and without grace and the resulting conditions of the soul. (This is fundamentally the gospel message, though to some extent, it applies to other close relationships as well.)

Contentment

Satisfaction with given conditions

Synonym: Happiness

Antonyms/obstacles: discontentment, complaining, whining, materialism, covetousness, avarice, grumbling, envy, jealousy

Imitations: complacency, positive thinking

Hesitation: Agreement that you are unworthy

Selected Verses

Ex. 20:17	Prov. 15:13	Isa. 45:9-12	Phil. 4:11-13
Numb. 21:4-6	Ecc. 3:12-13	Luke 3:14	1Thes. 5:16-18
Josh. 7	Ecc. 5:10	Rom. 8:28	1Tim. 6:6-10
1Kings 21	Ecc. 5:19-20	1Cor. 7:17	Heb. 13:5-6
Ps. 23:1	Ecc. 6:9	1Cor. 10:10	James 4:1-3
Prov. 14:30	Ecc. 7:14	Phil. 2:14-15	Jude 16

Memory Verses

"Do everything without complaining or arguing..."

Philippians 2:14

"I can do everything through him who gives me strength."

Philippians 4:13

Topic Introduction

Contentment means trying to make the best of what you have. Sometimes you have a lot and it seems like it would be easier to be happy; other times you do not have as much as other people do and it is harder. Either way though, God knows what is best for us and will take care of what we really need if we trust Him. It does not mean that we should not ask for things that we need or want; but if He (or anybody else) does not give it to us, we need to learn to do without it. Contentment finds the creative solution and sees the possibility in things that do not appear to be the best.

What is it like to be around people who are not content?

Literary Examples

<u>Short Stories</u>
"Billy Goats Gruff", Norwegian fairy tale
"The Fisherman and His Wife", Grimm brothers
"Gertrude McFuzz", *Yertle the Turtle and Other Stories*, Dr. Seuss
"The Golden Touch", Nathaniel Hawthorn
"It Could Always Be Worse", Margot Zemach
"The Knee-High Man", Julius Lester
"The Little Mermaid", Hans Christian Andersen
"Two of Everything", Alice Ritche

Collections

The Moral Compass:
  "The Cat and the Parrot"
  "The Discontented Pig"
  "The Discontented Stonecutter"
  "Fortune and the Beggar"
  "Grumble Family"
  "Grumble Town"
  "The King and the Shirt"
  "The Little Loaf"
  "Three Wishes"

Aesop:
  "The [Donkey] and His Masters"
  "The [Donkey] and the Lap Dog"
  "The Boy and the Filberts"
  "The Dog and the Shadow"
  "The Goose with the Golden Eggs"
  "The Milkmaid and Her Pail"
  "The Widow and the Hen"

McGuffey's Third Eclectic Reader:
  "The Contented Boy" (60)

McGuffey's Fourth Eclectic Reader:
  "Tomorrow" (11)
  "The Sailor's Consolation" (18)

Thomas the Tank Engine series:
  "Home at Last" (*The Little Old Engine*)
  "Passengers and Polish"
                (*Gallant Old Engine*)
  "Percy and the Trousers"
                (*Henry the Green Engine*)

Topic Analysis

Thought Provokers

❖ Discontentment is often an attitude of the heart, but sometimes it is more of a "spiritual discomfort" intended to motivate us to right some wrong. God will not *let* us be content with less than His best. So how can we tell when the discontentment has origins in selfishness or in the Spirit (for our actions are determined by the answer to this question)?

❖ How is complacency different from contentment?

❖ Does contentment require a sacrifice of vision? Does it require us to take a different path to different goals or to just accept a harder way to the same goals? Which goals can be compromised and which should never be?

❖ Is trying hard to find something for which to be positive really just a glossing over of truth and a compromise of your integrity? Does trying to be content force us to deny reality to some extent and settle for something superficial? If not, then what exactly does contentment do with harsh, unyielding circumstances?

❖ What is the difference between a complaint and a legitimate request? How can you tell the difference? How should we respond to each?

❖ Paul says that he has learned to be content in all circumstances, "whether well-fed or hungry, whether living in plenty or want" (Philippians 4:12). Does this imply that trying to relieve our suffering is wrong? Does this mean that problem-solving is selfish? Should we refuse aid when it is offered because suffering disciplines us better? What does he mean then?

❖ How is contentment closely connected to gratitude?

❖ "Less is more" is a common phrase that highlights contentment. When is this proverb true and when might it be misleading? When we must make do with less, what skills and character traits might we exercise that otherwise we would not?

Self-control

Overcoming emotional or physical impulses or temptations for a greater good

Synonyms: Moderation, Temperance, Self-restraint

Antonyms/obstacles: addiction, bad language, gluttony, drunkenness, obsession, impulsiveness, self-satisfaction

Imitations: moralism, asceticism

Hesitation: Un-quenched desires

Selected Verses

Gen. 4:6-7	Prov. 29:11	Rom. 8:6-8	2Tim. 4:5
Prov. 1:10-16	Ecc. 3:1-8	Rom. 13:14	Titus 2:2-12
Prov. 16:32	Matt. 18:7-9	Gal. 5:16-17	James 1:15
Prov. 23:4	Matt. 23:25	Col. 3:5-8	James 5:5
Prov. 23:29-35	Matt. 26:41	1Thes. 4:4	1Peter 1:13
Prov. 25:16-17	Rom. 6:14	1Thes. 5:6-8	1Peter 4:2-7
Prov. 25:28	Rom. 7:21-23	2Tim. 2:22	1Peter 5:8-9

Memory Verse

"No temptation has seized you
except what is common to man.
And God is faithful;
he will not let you be tempted beyond what you can bear."

1 Corinthians 10:13

Topic Introduction

Self-control is keeping ourselves from doing something that we know is bad-- even if we really want to do it. It can also be making ourselves to do something that we know is good, even if we do not want to. If we are going to be a self-controlled person, then we need to know two things: 1) what is right and good according to God and 2) what I want is not as right and good. We do the first by studying God's Word, hiding it in our heart, and listening to the Holy Spirit. The second, unfortunately, we have to learn from our mistakes-- and sometimes from seeing the mistakes of others. We also need to pay attention so we can see when there is a difference, because often we might both want the same thing! Just because we want something badly does not mean it is bad, it just means we should check what God has to say about it first. So self-control has a lot to do with thinking things through before we do them.

What happens to people who do not practice self-control?

Literary Examples

Collections

The Book of Virtues:
  "Self-Discipline"

The Moral Compass:
  "The Man without a Country"

McGuffey's Fifth Eclectic Reader:
  "The Venomous Worm" (17)
  "The Bobolink" (39)

Aesop:
  "The Mouse and the Weasel"

Activity Idea

❖ Make a jar full of small treats-- one for each day

Topic Analysis

Literary Examples
"From the Cabby's Seat", O. Henry
Moby Dick, Herman Melville
Othello, William Shakespeare
Sir Gawain and the Green Knight, Winny translation

❖ Much of self-control has to do with moderation. Snacking or relaxing or watching television are all activities that are fine in small quantities, but when left un-checked by our self-control, can become serious problems. What are some signs that we have crossed the line from enjoying a pleasant experience in our Christian freedom to becoming lax in our stewardship or responsibility?

❖ If we are not making an effort to control ourselves, at least being in the position to willfully make choices of who or what to follow, we are not truly free. There is always something or someone to fill the void we leave in neglecting self-control. What are some common ways people use to fill this void? Where is your weakness? How might these "control upsets" be remedied?

❖ Are self-control and zealousness often in opposition to each other? How can we know how far to apply each one?

❖ How is a healthy form of self-control different from a stoic philosophy (disconnecting emotions and do what you must)? How is having self-control different from being a moralist?

❖ There are many times when other people will reveal imperfections in our individual characters, intentionally or not. Certainly these can be helpful to opening our eyes and correcting flaws. So is it right to ever take offense? Surely there are some comments meant only to goad. How do we sift out which to ignore? What is an apt response that might defuse such comments?

❖ Self-control might be thought of as a sort of internal vigilance. We must carefully watch what we do and why we do it. And some of the very things that we are told *not* to judge in others, we must judge in ourselves. Make a mental note of an area in particular that poses a frequent temptation to you. What are two practical steps that you can take to temper the temptation or bolster your self-control when confronting it?

❖ Self-control is what we must apply to ignore an internal plea, with the purpose of achieving a greater good. However, internal pleas are not inherently wrong and are there for our protection, as early warning signals to potentially serious problems. So how far *should* we apply self-control in a given situation? If the urge dies shortly after our efforts to combat it, good. But what if it does not? Should we plan some way of addressing the plea responsibly?

❖ A frequent piece of advice in dealing with difficult situations is to respond, not react. What is the difference? What do we need to clearly understand to respond well? Jesus is such a beautiful and varied example of responding to others-- from a helpless invalid to a traitor. How did He view the encounters? How can we begin to see so clearly to know how to respond so well (even sometimes)?

Repentance

Acknowledgment and sincere expression of sorrow for a wrong done by you;
A turning from past ways

Synonyms: Penitence, Contrition

Antonyms/obstacles: excuses, self-justification

Imitation: regret

Hesitations: Exposes your guilt; Ensures unpleasant consequences

Selected Verses

Num. 32:23	Prov. 15:10	Matt. 4:17	Acts 20:21
Ps. 4:4	Prov. 15:31-32	Luke 3:8	Acts 26:20
Ps. 14:2-3	Prov. 28:13	Luke 5:31-32	Rom. 2:4-5
Ps. 32:1-5	Isa. 30:15	Luke 7:36-50	2Cor. 7:10
Ps. 38:1-18	Isa. 53:6	Luke 15:7-10	James 2:10
Ps. 51	Isa. 59:1-13	Luke 17:3	James 4:8-10
Prov. 3:11-12	Jer. 31:19	Luke 18:9-14	James 5:16
Prov. 10:17	Eze. 18:30-32	Luke 24:47	1Peter 3:11-12
Prov. 13:19	Joel 2:12-14	Acts 3:19	2Peter 3:9

Memory Verse

"If we confess our sins,
he is faithful and just
and will forgive us our sins
and purify us from all unrighteousness."

1 John 1:9

Topic Introduction

Repentance is the process of removing guilt. To begin, you must know what you did that was wrong. Then you must believe that it was wrong and that you are guilty. If you are sorry and want to turn away from its bad motivation, then finally you must express it to God, honestly. Jesus' death on the cross is the hope of our repentance. He has already paid the penalty, so we just need to wash our hands in Him. Repentance is freeing, akin to having a burden lifted off of us (for the burden of guilt is extremely heavy, gnawing away at our happiness). It places us back on the road to getting better instead of being destroyed. It is worth a little embarrassment. Let it go.

What is the ultimate destination of someone who completely refuses to repent?

Literary/Dramatic Examples

Short Story
The Tale of Two Bad Mice, Beatrix Potter

Drama
The Pirates of Penzance, Gilbert and Sullivan

Collections

The Moral Compass:
  "Nails in the Post"
  "The New Leaves"
  "The Night Wind"
  "Robert of Sicily"

McGuffey's Third Eclectic Reader:
  "The Truant" (7)

Thomas the Tank Engine series:
  "Rock 'n' Roll" (*The Little Old Engine*)
  "Useful Railway" (*Small Railway Engines*)

Additional Discussion Topics

❖ Saul's downfall (1 Samuel 13-15)
❖ Zacchaeus (Luke 19:1-9)
❖ St. Augustine
❖ Making amends
❖ Apologies

Topic Analysis

Literary and Dramatic Examples
Crime and Punishment, Fyodor Dostoyevsky
I Lombardi, Giuseppe Verdi (an opera)
"The Reformation of Calliope", O. Henry

Thought Provokers

- ❖ Why is it important to ask for forgiveness rather than just offering an apology for deep offenses? Describe how they are different. Does it matter if the infraction was accidental or intentional?

- ❖ How is confession closely connected to repentance? How do people sometimes separate them? Should there *ever* be one without the other?

- ❖ How far is restitution necessary in repentance? Certainly in practical matters, there must be some-- if only to prove the sincerity of the claim. But what about with God? Does enacting restitution necessarily imply repentance?

- ❖ What are things in general of which we need to repent? (Do not forget the negligence aspects.) Corporately, we are also guilty on numerous accounts. (Such as in Ezra 9:6-7.) How often should we repent of these? And how? We cannot possibly be perfectly aware of every infraction nor fight every injustice!

- ❖ Does repentance need forgiveness to be complete? What if the other person will not forgive? How does realizing that all offenses are really against God (Psalm 51:4) help solve this dilemma? Should we then continue to seek forgiveness from another, even when the case is spiritually "closed"?

- ❖ Regret alone can look a lot like repentance, and we can easily confuse them if we are not careful. What are some ways to distinguish the two? In ourselves? In another? (Job 34:31-33 may help clarify the difference.)

- ❖ Especially in close relationships, we can easily absorb the blame for another's wrongs. Can we apologize for someone else's behavior? (Is it possible, courteous, *and* right?) Can we repent for someone else's behavior? How do we deal with the shame and blame if we can neither control nor repent of it?! Can you serve another's penalty? Should we?

- ❖ What are the effects of long-term unrepentance? Often this can take the form of someone just pretending an offense never happened. What message does this convey to the offended party? Other times it looks like blatant sin. What message does this convey to God?

- ❖ What does repentance do if we still must suffer the consequences of our offense? Does refusing to justify ourselves leave us to the mercy/mercilessness of the ones who judge us, surrendering our own sense of justice? If repentance feels like too much of a risk, how can you ease the fears of someone who may need to apologize to you?

- ❖ For what sorts of things should we **not** repent? Cite an instance in Scripture where someone, in either direct or indirect obedience to God, caused someone else to suffer a blow (without lasting spiritual harm) which may be seen by many as requiring an apology or a retraction.

Kindness

Exhibition of openness of heart towards another

Synonyms: Encouragement, Benevolence, Blessing

Antonyms/obstacles: cruelty, gossip, sarcasm, hard-hardheartedness, malice, ridicule, discouragement

Imitation: pleasantness

Hesitation: Risk of being rejected

Selected Verses

Ezra 9:8–9	Prov. 27:17	Rom. 12:19–20	Titus 2:5
Prov. 11:16–17	Hosea 11:3–4	Gal. 6:10	Heb. 3:13
Prov. 12:25	Matt. 7:12	Col. 3:12–13	Heb. 10:25
Prov. 14:21	Matt. 10:41–42	1Thes. 4:18	2Peter 1:7
Prov. 14:31	Matt. 25:40	1Thes. 5:11	
Prov. 19:17	Luke 6:31–35	1Thes. 5:14–15	
Prov. 25:21–22	Acts 10	2Tim. 2:24–26	

Memory Verse

"Be kind and compassionate to one another,
forgiving each other, just as Christ God forgave you."

Ephesians 4:32

Topic Introduction

Kindness means showing someone that you care. If you really want someone to believe that you do care about him, you need to prove it by what you do: helping, hugging, giving, smiling, listening, praying, supporting. The best acts of kindness are those timed just right with what someone really needs, when he really needs it. Anything that perfect (though often not pretty) is good evidence of the Holy Spirit and powerful for everyone involved. Oddly enough, God often reserves us as the primary channel of His kindnesses. Even though it might not be well received, it is usually better to show you care than be sorry that you did not when you had the chance.

What would it be like if no one ever showed you any kindness?

Literary Examples

Literature
Black Beauty, Anna Sewell
The Family under the Bridge,
          Natalie Savage Carlson
The Little Princess, Frances Hodgson Burnett

Short Stories
The Little Engine That Could, Watty Piper
Make Way for Ducklings, Robert McCloskey

Hymn
"Little Drummer Boy",
          Katherine Kennicott Davis

Collections

The Moral Compass:
    "The Child's Story"
    "The Emerald Lizard"
    "The Hermit of the Himalayas"
    "I Sought My Soul"
    "The Lame Boy"
    "Mr. Straw"
    "The Princess Who Wanted to Be
          Beautiful"
    "The Tongue and How to Use It"
    "Two Gifts"
    "What Men Live By"
    "Why the Chimes Rang"

Aesop:
    "The Eagle and the Fox"

McGuffey's Third Eclectic Reader:
    "The Young Teacher" (10)
    "Deeds of Kindness" (49)

McGuffey's Fourth Eclectic Reader:
    "Smiles" (6)
    "Harry and His Dog" (27)
    "The Way to Be Happy" (59)

Thomas the Tank Engine series:
    "Duck Takes Charge"
          (Percy the Small Engine)
    "Special Funnel" *(Gallant Old Engine)*
    "Thomas and Bertie"
          (Tank Engine Thomas Again)

- ❖ Good Samaritan (Luke 10:30–37)
- ❖ Kindness to animals
- ❖ Stern kindness

Activity Ideas

- ❖ Do a "Random Acts of Kindness" campaign
- ❖ Write an encouraging note

Topic Analysis

Literary and Dramatic Examples

Anne of Green Gables, Lucy Maud Montgomery
La Cenerentola (Cinderella), Gioachino Rossini (an opera)
Oliver Twist, Charles Dickens
Silas Mariner, George Eliot
"The Trimmed Lamp", O. Henry

Thought Provokers

- ❖ Kindness is like taking a detour off your path of life to walk through the rough spots of someone else's with them. Make a "kindness" simile, too.
- ❖ How is being nice or pleasant different from being kind? What are the motivations of each? Give an example of how a nicety might be transformed into a kindness.
- ❖ What should we do when someone is *trying* to be kind to us, but is really just causing us more trouble? Does it make a difference how often this occurs? Does it matter who it is (e.g., their age or position)? Does it matter if they might take an honest confrontation badly?
- ❖ Kindness is mysteriously powerful. Cite one Biblical example of how kindness saved a life and one of how kindness resulted in persecution.
- ❖ Sometimes kindness is doing something the person will not like but is really for his greater good. God frequently applies this but, in general, we should do it sparingly. Who else would have the responsibility of applying this "stern kindness" more frequently? (What occupations require this and when?) How do we know when we should or should not?
- ❖ It has been said that you should forget the kindnesses you do for others but never forget the ones done for you. Why is this wise?
- ❖ One of the truest tests of a kindness is actually when it is rejected (where it is revealed *not* to be accomplishing a good). Are you offended by this revelation or are you willing to adjust your behavior to better bless the other? Give a real-life example of this contrast and what it implies.
- ❖ Sometimes the unexpected kindnesses are the most powerful (maybe because we clearly require the Divinity to do it through us). What kindness can you show to someone who does not deserve it, who does not expect it, or to whom you hardly know? Pray about it and then act on it within the next few days.

Responsibility

Fulfilling obligations well and in a timely manner

Synonyms: Dependability, Conscientiousness

Antonyms/obstacles: irresponsibility, negligence, recklessness, laziness, minimalism, procrastination

Imitation: control

Hesitations: Risk of being blamed; Risk of failure

Selected Verses

Gen. 2:15-16, 19-20	Prov. 19:18-19	Eze. 34:1-10	Gal. 6:4-5
Lev. 5:1	Prov. 20:4	Matt. 13:12	2Thes. 3:10-12
Ps. 8:3-8	Prov. 21:25-26	Luke 12:48b	1Tim. 5:8
Prov. 10:4-5	Prov. 22:15	Luke 13:6-9	2Tim. 2:25-26
Prov. 10:26	Prov. 23:13-14	Luke 14:25-35	Titus 3:14
Prov. 12:10-11	Prov. 24:30-34	Luke 17:1-3a	1Peter 4:10
Prov. 12:24	Prov. 27:18	John 10:1-15	
Prov. 14:23	Ecc. 11:6	Rom. 14:12	
Prov. 19:15	Eze. 33:1-9	1Cor. 4:1-2	

Memory Verse

"One who is slack in his work is brother to one who destroys."

Proverbs 18:9

Topic Introduction

Responsibility is taking care of the things that people are depending on you to do when they need to be done. As duty helps to meet valid wants, responsibility steps up to meet valid needs. The needs of a family or community are varied, but the responsibilities to meet them are usually divided according to ability. A toddler might only have responsibility for himself, but as he grows, he also has chores, a vehicle, and a job– all of which require regular and reliable care. So we each need to do our part so the whole can work at its best. And then, responsibility means that we have to answer for what we have done (or not done).

What happens when a job is not done responsibly?

Literary Examples

Literature
Boxcar Children, Gertrude Chandler Warner
Peter Pan, J. M. Barrie

Poetry
"Little Boy Blue", *The Real Mother Goose*

Collections

The Book of Virtues:
  "Responsibility"

The Moral Compass:
  "The Cost of One Seed"
  "Distance"
  "Ingratitude and Injustice of Men
                    Towards Fortune"
  "Mr. Nobody"
  "The Pig Brother"

Aesop:
  "The Ant and the Grasshopper"

McGuffey's Third Eclectic Reader:
  "The Money Amy Didn't Earn" (48)

McGuffey's Fourth Eclectic Reader:
  "Lazy Ned" (7)
  "Knowledge is Power" (56)

Additional Discussion Topics

- ❖ Privileges
- ❖ Holding others accountable
- ❖ Earning a living
- ❖ Living within your means (financial independence)
- ❖ Taxes
- ❖ Gambling

Topic Analysis

Literary Examples
The Adventures of Tom Sawyer, Mark Twain
"The Ransom of Red Chief", O. Henry
The Red Pony, John Steinbeck
The Sign of the Beaver, Elizabeth George Speare
The Wind in the Willows, Kenneth Grahame

Thought Provokers

- List things that you have or own and how you are responsible for them. We all have a weak link, so where might slackness have crept into your list? How might this be affecting others? Yourself? Your witness for God?

- Can we ever truly be responsible for anything if we do not have absolute control over it? Perhaps we can be responsible for ourselves, in as far as we have developed self-control. We may even be responsible for others, but only as far as we have authority to administer consequences. So where are we to take responsibility (hold a tight rein) and where are we to view ourselves as just stewards of God's property (hold a loose rein)?

- Intense burdens of responsibility can drive us to try to gain more control. What are some ways people try to gain more control, rightly and wrongly? When does trying to responsibly control situations and problems begin to violate others' freedoms?

- In what ways are we responsible to the previous generation? To the next generation? To the past and our heredity? To the future and our posterity? What does this look like practically?

- How do we distinguish between unnecessary obligations and real responsibilities? Surely we cannot be responsible for everything and everyone, but how far are we responsible to them? Similarly, how can we determine when a responsibility is dead and is no longer necessary?

- Being responsible tends to make people want to give you more responsibility. This can become a great honor or a huge burden. What is a responsible way of dealing with these "extras", especially if it turns into too much?

- "Ability + Opportunity + Motivation = Responsibility" is a good principle to follow for determining for what we need to be responsible and to hold others responsible. This helps distinguish laziness from real needs. When there is an ingredient missing and the responsibility still stands, we need to ask for help (or be willing to help another). Give an example of each --how ability, opportunity, and motivation individually can be missing from a responsibility.

- Jesus has some seemingly conflicting teachings on responsibility, such as His, "Follow Me, and let the dead bury their own dead" (Matthew 8:22). What does He mean by this?

Justice

Doing and accepting what is objectively right by God's law

Synonym: Fairness

Antonyms/obstacles: injustice, bias, partiality, revenge, leniency, license

Imitations: legalism, equality

Hesitation: Opens yourself to accusations, criticism, or opposition

Selected Verses

Dt. 16:18-20	Prov. 21:15	Amos 5:24	Col. 4:1
Dt. 27:19	Prov. 24:23-25	Luke 12:58-59	2Thes. 1:6-7
Ps. 106:3	Prov. 29:7	Rom. 1:18-22	1Tim. 5:21
Prov. 2:6-9	Ecc. 8:11-13	Rom. 2:6-11	Heb. 12:11
Prov. 3:27-30	Isa. 1:17	Rom. 6:23	James 2:1-9
Prov. 16:10	Isa. 30:18	2Cor. 8:21	1Peter 1:17
Prov. 17:15	Isa. 56:1	Gal. 6:7-8	
Prov. 21:3	Jer. 30:11	Col. 3:25	

Memory Verse

"He has showed you, O man, what is good.
And what does the Lord require of you?
To act justly and to love mercy
and to walk humbly with your God."

Micah 6:8

Topic Introduction

Justice is making sure that fair punishments are administered following wrongs committed. It means righting a wrong as far as it can be and trying to be sure that it does not happen again. It judges the action and its merit without considering one person as more important than another. Justice tries to understand what really happened. God, of course, is the only one who can judge perfectly and apply complete justice, but we need to do it as far as He has given us power. You always have power over yourself-- to avoid doing wrong, often you have influence with other people-- to judge fairly, and sometimes you have power over others (pets or people) -- to act with justice.

What does it feel like to be treated unjustly?

Literary Examples

Literature
The Magician's Nephew, C. S. Lewis

Detective Series
Boxcar Children, Gertrude Chandler Warner
Cam Jansen, David A. Adler
Encyclopedia Brown, Donald J. Sobol

Short Stories
Horton Hears a Who!, Dr. Seuss
The Story of Ping, Marjorie Flack
The Tale of Benjamin Bunny, Beatrix Potter

Collections

The Book of Virtues:
   "The Little Red Hen"

McGuffey's Fifth Eclectic Reader:
   "King Charles II and William Penn" (23)

Thomas the Tank Engine series:
   "The Sad Story of Henry"
        (The Three Railway Engines)

Additional Discussion Topics

❖ Purpose of laws, rules, and discipline
❖ Human rights
❖ Allowing natural consequences to bad behavior

Activity Idea

❖ Find just punishments for bad behavior

Topic Analysis

Thought Provokers

- Anger is largely produced by a perception of injustice, so it is a natural and healthy first warning sign. In wisdom, what are the following steps?

- Deuteronomy 19:21 says, "…eye for eye, tooth for tooth." How is this different from revenge? If you are responsible for administering (or even allowing) the consequences for a wrong done to yourself, how can you keep it from becoming revengeful?

- Jesus says to turn the other cheek and go an extra mile to those who are unkind to you. What does this have to do with justice? Is this a general principle to apply always, or only in certain situations?

- In general, we should be intolerant of injustice to others, but tolerate it to ourselves. But what if the other person does not realize he is being unfair or hurtful? How long should we remain in silence? And what should be the first steps for dealing with it once we are determined to address the issue? (What are the cues that we need to begin exerting our rights?)

- How is justice different from fairness or equality? To clarify, God is certainly perfectly just, but He is also clearly not fair in His distribution of abilities, resources, or opportunities. How can we strive for justice without being caught in the trap of keeping everything perfectly "fair"?

- Law is intended to administer justice, but sometimes following the letter of the law will result in unjust suffering. What is an example of this? How are we to determine when to apply "the letter of the law" and when to apply "the spirit of the law"?

- What if a tyrant just keeps increasing the oppression to you to the point that it becomes unbearable? Perhaps he does not realize what he is doing, though more likely he does. What should you do as the oppressed, especially over a long period of time? (e.g., African slaves, Holocaust prisoners) Does it matter if you are alone or suffering as a group?

- What can a person do when he is faced with blatant injustice, where reasonable argument is completely dismissed? What is the next step?

- In a position of authority, it is important to clearly state the consequences of disobedience. While specific consequences may vary, they must be consistently applied and the degree of severity must be proportional to the offense. What happens when the consequences are not stated? Or if the punishment is normally too light? Too severe? Arbitrary?

- When administering justice, you may be accused of a wide variety of things: from legalism to prejudice to cruelty. What is a good way to dispel these accusations? How can you maintain a solid objectivity that will help to reaffirm your authority?

Mercy

Deferring suffering because of the weakness of another

Synonyms: Compassion, Sympathy, Clemency

Antonyms/obstacles: indifference, blame, legalism, uncompromisingness, revenge, condemnation

Imitation: leniency

Hesitation: Accusations of injustice

Selected Verses

2Kings 6:8-23	Joel 2:13	Matt. 9:12-13	Eph. 4:32
Neh. 9:17	Hosea 6:6	Matt. 9:36	Col. 3:12
Ps. 41:1-3	Micah 6:8	Luke 6:36-37	Titus 3:5
Ps. 103:4-13	Micah 7:19-20	John 8:2-11	James 2:12-13
Isa. 1:18	Zec. 7:9	Rom. 12:15	1Peter 3:7-9
Isa. 49:13	Matt. 5:7	Rom. 14:1-4	Jude 22-23
Isa. 54:4-10	Matt. 7:1-5	Rom. 14:13	

Memory Verse

"...his compassions never fail.
They are new every morning;
great is your faithfulness."

Lamentations 3:22b-23

Topic Introduction

Mercy is rescuing someone from pain. It sees that what a person is suffering through is more than he can bear and that you have the ability to help relieve it, even a little. Often we have the strongest desire to help when we remember suffering from a similar problem; so our own suffering opens our eyes to recognize it in others. It also helps us to know the best way to help. "Be merciful, just as your Father is merciful" (Luke 6:36). Mercy is rescue from an overwhelming problem by someone who understands. Even if we deserve to suffer, true mercy is the fingerprint of God.

Why do you think God is more merciful to us if we have shown mercy to others?

Literary Examples

Short Stories
"Beauty and the Beast", traditional fairy tale
"Snow White and the Seven Dwarfs",
                              Grimm brothers
The Tailor of Gloucester, Beatrix Potter
The Three Robbers, Tomi Ungerer
"Tilly's Christmas", Louisa May Alcott

Hymn
"Come, Thou Fount", Robert Robinson

Collections

The Book of Virtues:
   "Compassion"

The Moral Compass:
   "Grief"
   "A Pioneer of Compassion"
   "Pocahontas"
   "The Student"

Aesop:
   "The Lion and the Mouse"

McGuffey's Third Eclectic Reader:
   "The Birds Set Free" (19)

McGuffey's Fourth Eclectic Reader:
   "The Lost Child" (61)

Thomas the Tank Engine series:
   "Coal" *(Henry the Green Engine)*
   "Double Header"
                    (The Eight Famous Engines)
   "Escape" *(Enterprising Engines)*
   "Saved from Scrap"
                    (Edward the Blue Engine)

Topic Analysis

Thought Provokers

- ❖ "Mercy is like a kitchen towel." Expound this simile or create your own and describe the similarities.

- ❖ Mercy is more than just a sympathetic identification with the sufferer in that it sometimes requires action (James 2:17), if possible. At the same time however, we cannot right every injustice that we encounter. How should we judge how far and when to get involved in extending aid to someone who is suffering?

- ❖ How do you know when a person should receive justice and when he should receive mercy?

- ❖ Is sympathy a thing that can be earned or a right to be claimed? If we believe that we have suffered enough already, have completely repented, or were excusably ignorant, are we justified in expecting mercy or compassion? Should we go out of our way to seek it out? Should we compel others to offer it? Or is a demand for mercy really just evidence that we are not yet in the condition to truly receive it?

- ❖ Sometimes if a person is sinning, he is suffering from the consequences of his sin. In this case, sympathy is highly inappropriate and even hinders God's work. A greater mercy is to chastise. How do we know when to apply this? And for how long and to what degree?

- ❖ How is pity different from mercy? How is leniency different from mercy?

- ❖ What is a man without mercy? Considering the particularly horrific events of oppression in history (i.e., concentration camps), what becomes of each side: the oppressed who receive no mercy and the oppressor who refuses to offer any? What does this say about it?

- ❖ Should we ever refuse sympathy when it is offered? Describe a situation where it might be appropriate to decline it.

- ❖ Sometimes mercy comes in the form of giving someone the benefit of the doubt. In some ways, this helps protect us from the embarrassment and consequences of hasty, erroneous judgments. There can come a point however where the doubts are worn thin with repeated episodes of a certain behavior. Is withdrawing your sympathy in this case really a sign of weakness, fickleness, or hard-heartedness-- as you will likely be accused? What is the greater need in this case?

Respect

Upholding the dignity of others in attitude and action;
Treating others as if they are important

Synonym: Reverence

Antonyms/obstacles: disrespect, rudeness, sarcasm, ridicule, contempt, impertinence, impoliteness, insolence, meddling

Imitations: appeasement, idolization

Hesitation: Risk in appearing inferior

Selected Verses

Lev. 19:3	Ps. 89:7	Matt. 7:12	1Thes. 5:12–13
Lev. 19:32	Prov. 11:16	Mark 12:30–31	1Tim. 6:1–2
Deut. 13:4	Ecc. 3:14	Eph. 5:21	Titus 2:2–3
Deut. 17:18–20	Ecc. 10:20	Eph. 6:4–5	1Peter 1:17
2Kings 2:23–25	Isa. 6:1–8	Col. 3:21–22	1Peter 3:1–7
Job 37:21–24	Matt. 5:21–22	1Thes. 4:11–12	1Peter 3:15

Memory Verse

"Show proper respect to everyone:
Love the brotherhood of believers,
fear God, honor the king."

1 Peter 2:17

Topic Introduction

Respect means that you value someone or something and show it by your actions. You respect things that are important to you by treating them with care so they will last a long time. Toys are picked up so they will not get broken, gardens are weeded so that they will not be choked out, homes are repaired so they will not collapse. But it is even more important for people. We are to treat all people with respect because they are made in the image of God. We are each a unique treasure to Him. And we should especially respect people who have shown themselves to be like Jesus-- good or wise or kind.

What happens when you do not show respect to someone who deserves it?

Literary Examples

Literature
Alice's Adventures in Wonderland, Lewis Carroll
Sounder, William H. Armstrong

Short Stories
Cat in the Hat, Dr. Seuss
"Goldilocks and the Three Bears",
English fairy tale
"Onawandah", Louisa May Alcott
"Ugly Duckling", Hans Christian Andersen
What Do You Say, Dear?, Sesyle Joslin

Collections

The Moral Compass:
    "Rules of Behavior"

McGuffey's Third Eclectic Reader:
    "A Walk in the Garden" (12)
    "The Insolent Boy" (62)
    "The Pert Chicken" (72)

McGuffey's Fourth Eclectic Reader:
    "Meddlesome Matty" (9)
    "The Good Son" (10)

McGuffey's Fifth Eclectic Reader:
    "Do Not Meddle" (7)

Thomas the Tank Engine series:
    "Henry's Sneeze" *(Henry the Green Engine)*
    "Old Iron" *(Edward the Blue Engine)*
    "Thomas and Gordon"
        (Thomas the Tank Engine)

Additional Discussion Topics

❖ Manners
❖ Courtesy
❖ Politeness

Activity Idea

❖ Play "Mother, May I" game

Topic Analysis

"The Duplicity of Hargraves", O. Henry
"The Gettysburg Address", Abraham Lincoln
Poor Folk, Fyodor Dostoevsky
"Thimble, Thimble", O. Henry
To Kill a Mockingbird, Harper Lee

Thought Provokers

- ❖ It is commonly said that respect is something that must be earned. On what levels is this true? When should we show respect for others regardless of their behaviors?

- ❖ Respect of a person can go too far and become idolization. What are the signs that it has crossed this line? How can this end up devastating the one whom you are trying to respect? Your relationship with God?

- ❖ One of the great difficulties of life is showing respect to a person without respecting/ supporting his wrong behaviors or beliefs. Cite a Biblical example of someone who faced such a situation. How does this guide us in handling such a dilemma?

- ❖ What is the difference between respect and fear? Where are the differences particularly vague? Are there different degrees of fear, some of which we are called to have and some we are not?

- ❖ In many situations, especially where it is required frequently, respect can become cool and rigid. How do we know when to maintain a formal respect and when to incorporate some level of sincerity? Many people, particularly in their relationships with God, habitually lean towards one side or the other. What do the extremes cost, and how do we maintain a good balance?

- ❖ Part of showing respect to another is being flexible, being willing to become like them in some ways and avoiding causing offense. Paul explains his efforts in this regard in 1 Corinthians 9:19-23. But part of showing respect is by *not* compromising on certain fast truths and principles. List those you need to hold to regardless what it might cost you or how much you might shame or offend another.

- ❖ Another aspect of respect is overlooking imperfections-- those little lapses in others that cause them embarrassment or may easily be misunderstandings on our own part. Certainly grace smoothes over the little inconsistencies that plague us all, and we are required to extend that same grace to others. But when do the little violations add up to a chronic problem that ought to be addressed? Practically, what is a good strategy for respectfully confronting the problem?

❖ When we must deal with particularly unpleasant people (usually the ones who do not know how to respect *you*), respect is very difficult. The easy answer is to just appease them when they are watching you to avoid an ugly conflict. But is this really showing respect, especially if it is a regular occurrence? What is a more respectful approach? And if that does not work-- is it appropriate (and even ultimately most respectful) to resort to risking an ugly scene?

❖ To some extent, respect must be adjusted to the individual. What might be considered respectful towards one person can become disrespectful when applied to another person-- or even to the same person in another stage of life. (Consider the ill or the aging or those with poor judgment.) Give an example of this. How are we to come to understand what is and is not respectful for an individual then?

Perseverance

Proceeding despite circumstances beyond your control

Synonyms: Long-Suffering, Endurance, Fortitude, Resolution

Antonyms/obstacles: shortsightedness, stubbornness, self-pity

Imitation: coping

Hesitation: Risk of exhaustion

Selected Verses

Prov. 13:11	Luke 14:27	Phil. 3:13-14	1Peter 2:20-24
Prov. 20:30	Luke 18:2-8	Heb. 12:1-12	1Peter 3:14-18
Prov. 24:10	John 8:31-32	James 1:2-4	1Peter 4:1
Matt. 5:10-12	Rom. 5:3-4	James 1:12	1Peter 4:12-19
Mark 13:5-13	Rom 12:12	James 5:10-11	1Peter 5:9-10
Luke 11:5-8	Gal. 6:12-13	1Peter 1:6-7	

Memory Verse

"Endure hardship with us like a good soldier of Christ Jesus."

2 Timothy 2:3

Topic Introduction

Perseverance is the determination to keep trudging through the storms. Problems, misunderstandings, complications, and disasters are all things that each of us will face no matter what we do in life. But the good news is that they are not there just to make us suffer. Suffering, though often part of the process, is **not** God's end goal for you. The difficulties are challenges to be met with the help and wisdom of the Holy Spirit. They stretch us, they hone us, they strengthen us, they teach us. And once they are overcome, they can make us even more certain of God's great love, power, and creativity at work in our lives right now. So keep pressing on!

What happens to the work of those who do not persevere?

Literary Examples

Literature
Carry On, Mr. Bowditch, Jean Lee Latham

Short Stories
Green Eggs and Ham, Dr. Seuss
Katy No-Pockets, Emmy Payne
"Rumpilstilskin", Grimm brothers

Collections

The Book of Virtues:
　"Perseverance"

The Moral Compass:
　"The Gordian Knot"

Aesop:
　"The Creaking Wheels"

McGuffey's Third Eclectic Reader:
　"Castle Building" (4-5)

McGuffey's Fourth Eclectic Reader:
　"Perseverance" (1)
　"Try, Try Again" (2)
　"The Old Eagle Tree" (30)

Thomas the Tank Engine series:
　"Bulldog" *(Duke the Lost Engine)*
　"Edward's Exploit" *(Main Line Engines)*
　"Gallant Old Engine" *(Gallant Old Engine)*
　"Triple-Header" *(Really Useful Engines)*
　"Troublesome Trucks"

　　　　　(James the Red Engine)

Additional Discussion Topic

❖ Job (Job 1-2)

Topic Analysis

Literary Examples

The Grapes of Wrath, John Steinbeck
"The Halberdier of the Little Rheinschloss", O. Henry
Kidnapped, Robert Louis Stevenson
Where the Red Fern Grows, Wilson Rawls

Thought Provokers

❖ Often we must persevere through what we cannot change. But sometimes we must try to change what we can no longer endure. Therefore, it can sometimes look like waiting and sometimes look like arbitrary trial and error. So the application of perseverance requires some degree of wisdom. How do we weigh which approach is more vital?

❖ When we are in pain (physical, emotional, etc.), the first step to problem-solving is to identify its source. What are the following steps, and where does perseverance fall in place? (It may be helpful to think of a specific problem, such as loud music coming regularly from a neighboring apartment late at night.) What would happen if you bypass the other steps, for whatever reason, and went straight to perseverance? What negative results might needless suffering (in the name of perseverance) incur? Alternatively, what might happen if someone gets stuck on one of the earlier steps, without ever progressing?

❖ When someone is following a harmful path, God will send warnings, obstacles, and consequences to draw them back. In some ways, it may appear that proceeding despite the set-backs caused by discipline is admirable, when it is simply rebellious. Like diligence versus stubbornness, how can you distinguish between perseverance and rebellion?

❖ The sturdiest toys are not those built to "never break," but those that are designed to be easily repaired when they do break. How does knowing when and where to yield relate to perseverance? Is taking a break helpful or harmful to perseverance?

❖ Often those who have to endure long struggles develop "coping methods" for dealing with their problems. Is this necessarily the same as persevering or might they be antagonistic to it? If not, what is a better approach?

❖ Persevering in standing up for anything requires sacrifice. All sorts of people-- religious or not-- will sacrifice even in horrific ways to persevere in what they believe is good. While in some ways, this may appear admirable; really many are fighting *against* God. (e.g., Saul/Paul) How can we determine on which side we are? Is checking periodically necessarily a sign of doubting or shaken faith?

❖ Life is always a struggle, in one way or another. One way to build perseverance is to remember how the Lord suffered in His life here. Make a list of the hardships He had to endure and the sufferings He experienced. Are your struggles on His list too?

Joy

A gladness and energy for good that is beyond circumstances

Antonyms/obstacles: despair, resignation, drudgery

Imitation: warm emotions

Hesitation: Risk of rousing resentment in others

Selected Verses

Neh. 8:10	Ecc. 8:15	Luke 19:1-9	2Cor. 6:10
Ps. 35:9	Isa. 35	John 6:27	1Thes. 5:16
Ps. 100:1-2	Jer. 15:16	John 15:11	1Thes. 5:19
Prov. 15:15	Hab. 3:17-18	Rom. 5:2	Heb. 12:2
Prov. 15:30	Mark 2:18-22	Rom. 12:12	James 1:2-4
Prov. 17:22	Luke 10:20	Rom. 15:13	Rev. 19:7

Memory Verse

"Rejoice in the Lord always.
I will say it again: Rejoice!"

Philippians 4:4

Topic Introduction

Joy means that you are so certain that you are working towards some great and wonderful goal that you will gladly keep working at it even when things might not be going so well. And often the goal, though you may not realize it, is just to appreciate the goodness of God that is revealed in His creation. It may not be something you always feel, but it is something you should see in your mind. Sometimes we do feel it though-- when we can see bits of the goal becoming real. The greatest joys join our efforts with God's purpose so that we are whisked along by the Holy Spirit and can see all sorts of good fruit and pockets of beauty appearing all around us. Do you want to have a joy like that?!

What does a person who has no joy look like?

Literary Examples

Literature
Little House series, Laura Ingalls Wilder
The Railway Children, Edith Nesbit

Short Stories
The Grinch Who Stole Christmas, Dr. Seuss

Hymns
"Joyful, Joyful, We Adore Thee",
Henry van Dyke
"This is My Father's World",
Maltbie Davenport
"Turn Your Eyes upon Jesus",
Helen H. Lemmel

Collections

McGuffey's Fourth Eclectic Reader:
   "Piccola" (13)
   "How Margery Wondered" (35)
   "The Fountain" (41)
   "The Nettle" (44)

Additional Discussion Topics

❖ J-O-Y acronym (**J**esus, **O**thers, **Y**ourself): If others dominate, it becomes a groaning "Oooh". If I dominate, it becomes a big "Why?" If Jesus dominates, it has the "us" in it already.

❖ Christian versus non-Christian funerals

Topic Analysis

Literary Examples
The Giver, Lois Lowry
The Hiding Place, Corrie ten Boom
"The Skylight Room", O. Henry

Thought Provokers

- ❖ How is joy similar to happiness? How is it different? (Use plenty of adjectives.)
- ❖ Paul says that we should "[b]e joyful always" (1 Thessalonians 5:16), suggesting that joy is more of a mindset than an emotion. Of what truth should we be reminding ourselves in order to remain joyful-- or is there some other way of controlling our joy?
- ❖ How might joy be closely connected to hope? How is it connected to clearer vision and deeper insight?
- ❖ What are some of the effects a joyful person has on a difficult situation? How is this different from optimism?
- ❖ James says that we should "[c]onsider it pure joy, my brothers, whenever you face trials of many kinds" (James 1:2). Certainly we do not *enjoy* the troubles and *should* try to solve them-- so how can we have joy without enjoyment? What are we to see beyond the circumstances?
- ❖ It has been said that deep and lasting friendships result in shared joys. If joys are the deep, personal things that bring us satisfaction, how might this be an even stronger bond than those of mutual sorrow or a common cause in conflict? What does this say about the Body of Christ?
- ❖ Joy, as one of the fruits of the Spirit, should be a sign of reassurance that you are working within the Lord's will. Work-- however logically noble and self-sacrificial-- must be achieving a greater good than if you did not work. So can you have joy if you do not have confidence that what you are doing *is* for the best? How can we realign our energies to have more joy?
- ❖ Sometimes, the key to knowing deep joy is knowing deep sorrow. How have you seen this to be true? What other paths to true joy have you observed?
- ❖ Joy is one of the most elusive virtues but also one of the most powerful witnesses. How has the evidence of true joy influenced your walk with Christ?

Trustworthiness

Able to be depended upon without expressed direction

Synonyms: Reliability, Credibility, Soundness

Antonyms/obstacles: unreliability, bribery

Imitation: consistency

Hesitation: Increase in demands or expectations

Selected Verses

Ex. 18:20-23	Prov. 11:13	Matt. 21:28-31	1Cor. 9:17
Ex. 23:1-8	Prov. 13:17	Matt. 28:11-15	1Tim. 3:2-11
Deut. 16:19	Prov. 15:27	Luke 3:7-14	2Tim. 2:2
1Sam. 27:1-12	Prov. 25:13	Luke 12:42-48	Titus 2:9-10
2Kings 5:15-27	Prov. 27:6	Luke 16:10-12	James 3:1-6
Neh. 13:12-13	Prov. 31:10-12	Luke 19:11-26	Rev. 22:6
Prov. 3:29-30	Dan. 6:4-5	Luke 20:9-19	

Memory Verse

"'Whoever can be trusted with very little
can also be trusted with much,
and whoever is dishonest with very little
will also be dishonest with much.'"

Luke 16:10

Topic Introduction

Trustworthiness means that you can be trusted, not only that you can follow directions well but that you can also make good judgments when something unexpected happens. Trustworthy people understand what the goal of the job is, so that they can adjust as necessary to best reach it. They care about doing a job well and are willing to use their time, energy, and imagination to see it through. Being trustworthy can also apply to guarding truth. A trustworthy saying can be believed because it is founded on truth-- it is stable, sound, and certain. Likewise, a trustworthy person is founded on the Truth in the Word of God.

What happens when we trust something that is untrustworthy?

Literary Examples

Literature
Shiloh, Phyllis Reynolds Naylor

Graphic Book
The Adventures of Tintin (any), Herge

Short Stories
"The Boy at the Dike", *Hans Brinkner; or, The Silver Skates*, Mary Mapes Dodge
"Rikki-Tikki-Tavi", *Jungle Book*, Rudyard Kipling

Collections

The Book of Virtues:
"Cat and Mouse in Partnership"

Aesop:
"The Boy Who Cried 'Wolf'"
"The Fox and the Crow"

Thomas the Tank Engine series:
"Edward's Day Out"
(The Three Railway Engines)
"Sir Handel" *(Four Little Engines)*

Additional Discussion Topics

❖ Attention to detail
❖ Punctuality
❖ Common sense
❖ Quality in craftsmanship versus cutting corners

Activity Idea

❖ Credibility game (blindfolded person must reach a goal by following directions of shouting people-- only one of which is telling the truth)

Topic Analysis

Literary Examples
King Lear, William Shakespeare
Old Yeller, Fred Gipson
"The Open Window", H. H. Munro

Thought Provokers

- ❖ How is trustworthiness different from faithfulness? How is it alike?
- ❖ Trustworthiness is proved best through the little things. What would be a good way to test for this in an interview process?
- ❖ Compare and contrast consistency and trustworthiness.
- ❖ What does it mean to be worthy of kindness or worthy of grace? How are these different from being worthy of trust? How can we "become" worthy of receiving some blessings but not of receiving others?
- ❖ How might over-optimism become an obstacle to trustworthiness? Is it worth it, considering how hard it is to regain trust once it is lost? What then builds trust better?
- ❖ It has been said that love is freely given but trust must be earned. Why is this wise? What does this require of us?
- ❖ Sometimes (though not habitually or sinfully) standing up for what is right will require us to break a law, a promise, a confidence, or some other human bond. How does this apparent violation of trust ultimately establish your trustworthiness? Cite a Biblical figure who had to face such a dilemma.
- ❖ What other virtues might people display that suggests that they are trustworthy? Does this vary according to a person's perspective? Is there some more objective means of evaluating another's reliability when you are just establishing a relationship? How far should we trust others when we first meet them?
- ❖ Is something necessarily (or even usually) trustworthy because it appears the intellectual argument or evidence for it is sound? When should we take the initiative to dig deeper and when should we "just take their word for it"?
- ❖ Ultimately, trustworthiness is based on the firmness of one's foundation on the Rock. This, at times, can be tricky to judge however. Though there is no empirical measure, how might the frequency of Jesus' "surprise visits" through him be a good indication of a man's trustworthiness? Cite an example of a person you trust precisely because his trust is in the Right Place.

Loyalty

Defending a person or cause despite the imperfections and possible shame

Synonyms: Dedication, Devotion, Allegiance

Antonyms/obstacles: disloyalty, treason, betrayal

Imitations: bias, fanaticism, close-mindedness

Hesitations: Accusation of prejudice or foolishness; Embarrassment in failure

Selected Verses

Gen. 25:5-9	1Sam. 19:8-17	Prov. 17:17	Mark 16:1-3
Gen. 45:1-15	1Sam. 20	Prov. 27:10	Luke 14:26
Ex. 32:7-14	1Sam. 24	Hosea 3:1-3	Luke 16:13
Ruth 1:1-19	1Sam. 26	Matt. 26:14-16, 27:1-5	
1Sam. 18:1-4	Esth. 2:19-23	Matt. 26:31-56	Acts 15:36-40
1Sam. 19:1-7	Ps. 109:1-4	Matt. 27:57-60	Rom. 12:10

Memory Verse

"'In the same way,
any of you who does not give up everything he has
cannot be my disciple.'"

Luke 14:33

Topic Introduction

Loyalty is supporting another (person, group, or cause) even though they are not perfect. Sometimes that means that you have to look foolish so that your friend does not have to stand alone. Sometimes it means that you overlook minor problems and find ways to work around them. Sometimes it means speaking up for a friend or giving him the benefit of the doubt, even if you do not completely understand the problem. Loyalty requires a confidence in the other that is stronger than your own comfort. But we have to be careful where we pledge our loyalty too-- though with God, you cannot go wrong.

What does it feel like when someone fails to be loyal when he should have been?

Literary Examples

Literature
Incredible Journey, Sheila Burnford
Princess Bride, William Goldman
Velveteen Rabbit, Margery Williams

Short Pieces
"Mowgli's Brothers", *Jungle Book,*
Rudyard Kipling
"The Pledge of Allegiance"

Hymn
"I Have Decided to Follow Jesus",
S. Sundar Singh

Collections

The Book of Virtues:
   "Loyalty"

The Moral Compass:
   "The Dog of Montargis"
   "Maid of Orleans",
   "The Man without a Country"
   "The Wounded Pine Tree"

Aesop:
   "The Bear and the Travelers"
   "The Belly and the Other Members"
   "The Birds, the Beasts, and the Bat"
   "The Bundle of Sticks"
   "The Goatherd and the Goats"

McGuffey's Fourth Eclectic Reader:
   "Brandywine Ford" (85-86)

Additional Discussion Topic

❖ Marriage

Topic Analysis

Literary and Dramatic Examples

Aida, Giuseppe Verdi (an opera)

All the Pretty Horses, Cormac McCarthy

"A Call Loan", O. Henry

"A Cosmopolite in a Café", O. Henry

"Friends in San Rosario", O. Henry

Greyfriar's Bobby, Eleanor Atkinson

"The Lady, or the Tiger?", Frank Stockton

The Scarlet Pimpernel, Baroness Orczy

"Telemachus, Friend", O. Henry

The Three Musketeers, Andre Dumas

The Two Gentlemen of Verona,

William Shakespeare

Thought Provokers

- ❖ Biblical loyalty is a belief in a Person more than in an ideal or creed. Do a Bible survey of "believe in Me". In what context is this phrase usually found?

- ❖ What is the difference between loyalty and prejudice? Loyalty and bias? Loyalty and dependency? Loyalty and fanaticism? Loyalty and identity?

- ❖ Consistency is considered an admirable trait and is very important in many regards (particularly for people in positions of authority). But loyalty to a person sometimes requires you to become inconsistent in other areas. Cite a Biblical figure whose behavior appears inconsistent, or even unstable, in response to loyal service to God.

- ❖ When our loyalties are divided, how are we to choose a side? Maintain a neutral stance? Is diplomacy an obstacle or an aid to loyalty?

- ❖ Loyalty to a human being means that we uphold the real person, not just an idealized image we may have of him (or want him to have). Parent-teacher conferences are a good illustration of this: parents are to be loyal to their child, but not at the expense of excusing or denying truth (as presented by the teacher). So how can we be gracefully loyal without undermining the truth?

- ❖ When must loyalty to a person/group be overridden by loyalty to a cause? Certainly the Confederate soldiers had admirable loyalty to their people during the American Civil War, but ultimately their cause was unjust to a third party. How are we to judge where to pledge our allegiance?

- ❖ Is loyalty to a cause, above your reputation, wise? Above your own safety, noble? How can we judge when it is? How can we judge when our loyalty ceases to promote good and begins just to enable evil?

- ❖ Loyalty requires commitment. This may often lead to unpleasant sacrifice or suffering. When is it appropriate to "burn our bridges behind us" to motivate ourselves to remain loyal, and when is it a foolish thing to limit our options? Give an example of each.

- ❖ Motivation for loyalty is usually either obligation or devotion. Devotion based on solid trustworthiness is of course best, but is that based on obligation necessarily wrong? When is it wrong?

- ❖ Does loyalty to a person necessarily mean that we must overlook his wrong choices? Does it mean we must necessarily correct the mistakes he makes at our own cost? Does it mean we should emphatically confront the behavior to make him right? What *does* it mean to be loyal to someone, without having to compromise our own integrity? Can the same explanation be used to describe loyalty to a cause?

❖ How far is mutuality necessary to loyalty? If a person or organization ceases to be loyal to you, is it wise to cease to be loyal to them? Consider employer-employee as well as parent-child relations. What are the conditions for loyalty then?

Forgiveness

Letting go of the anger due another for a wrong committed

Synonyms: Redemption, Pardon

Antonyms/obstacles: begrudging, blaming, bitterness, revenge

Imitation: excusing

Hesitation: Leaves you no right to a defensive argument against your offender

Selected Verses

Gen. 33:1-15	Isa. 43:25	Luke 11:4	1Cor. 6:1-8
Lev. 19:18	Isa. 44:22	Luke 15:11-32	Eph. 4:26-27
Ps. 32:1-2	Isa. 55:6-7	Luke 17:3-5	Eph. 4:31-32
Ps. 103:9-12	Matt. 6:14-15	Luke 23:34	Col. 3:13
Prov. 12:16	Matt. 18:21-35	Acts 3:19	1John 1:9
Prov. 17:9	Mark 11:25	Acts 7:54-60	
Prov. 20:22	Luke 6:37	Rom. 12:14	
Isa. 38:17	Luke 7:36-48	Rom. 12:17-21	

Memory Verse

"'Though your sins are like scarlet,
they shall be as white as snow;
though they are red as crimson,
they shall be like wool.'"

Isaiah 1:18

Topic Introduction

Forgiveness means that we promise not to hurt the person who has hurt us. We can still think what they did was wrong, we can still hurt inside, and we can still watch out for more of their trouble, but forgiveness does not repay a wrong. This is very hard to do when things are not fair, but Jesus knows it is for our best. He knows how badly it can hurt to be hated, teased, and spat upon, yet He was still willing to **die** so that the Father would be able to completely forgive. We should be willing to forgive too and leave all the correcting-the-unfair bits to God.

What happens to a person who refuses to forgive?

Literary/Dramatic Examples

Literature
The Tale of Despereaux, Kate DiCamillo

Ballet
The Nutcracker, Pyotr Ilyich Tchaikovsky

Short Story
Reuben and the Quilt, Merle Good

Collections

The Book of Virtues:
   "Little Girls Wiser Than Men"

The Moral Compass:
   "The Man Who Broke the Color Barrier"

Aesop:
   "The Horse and the Stag"
   "Jupiter and the Bee"

McGuffey's Fourth Eclectic Reader:
   "The Noblest Revenge" (33)
   "The Dying Soldiers" (82)

Thomas the Tank Engine series:
   "Edward, Gordon, and Henry"
                   (The Three Railway Engines)
   "Tenders and Turntables"
                      (Troublesome Engines)

Additional Discussion Topics

- ❖ Joseph and his brothers (Genesis 37, 42-45)
- ❖ Illustration of forgiveness as putting out a fire with water, not more fire

Topic Analysis

Literary and Dramatic Examples

Ben-Hur, Lew Wallace
The Count of Monte Cristo, Alexander Dumas
"The Cask of Amontillado", Edgar Allan Poe
La Clemenza di Tito, Wolfgang Amadeus Mozart (an opera)
The Mill on the Floss, George Eliot
Wuthering Heights, Emily Bronte

Thought Provokers

❖ Forgiveness is often mistaken for many things: forgetfulness, foolish trust, denial, excusing, justifying. But it might be best described as a "letting go" -- but a "letting go" of what? And how does this look practically, especially when the hurt still rankles?

❖ How can we forgive even when the other is not sorry or is unreachable? How can we forgive when we know that we are certain to be violated again and again in the same manner? Can forgiveness become a license to abuse without repercussions? Presumably not, but what can you do to make that distinction clear to the offender?

❖ What is the difference between divine forgiveness and human forgiveness? How does knowing how much we are forgiven motivate us best to forgive others?

❖ What should forgiveness do about the consequences of the offense? Should we ever demand retribution? For ourselves? For others? Should we accept retribution if it is offered?

❖ What behaviors might characterize someone who has forgiven in contrast to someone who has not? (Be careful not to confuse it with a foolish trust.) Make a list.

❖ Once we have been dealt an offensive blow, our first step (after we overcome the shock) is to evaluate whether the blow was just or not. If it was unjust, then "letting it go" in forgiveness is absolutely in order. If the blow was just, "letting it go" is really not appropriate, and we should follow the path of repentance. (Though many times it can be a blend of the two.) Describe what might be the consequences if we are hasty to forgive (or repent) without first honestly judging the justice of the claim.

❖ Write a "recipe for forgiveness". (Include steps from the hurt through to the end, with virtues and attitudes to include along the way.)

Gentleness

Calm and mild in tone and manner towards others

Synonym: Tenderness

Antonyms/obstacles: cruelty, harshness, temper, cynicism

Imitation: timidity

Hesitation: Risk of being viewed as a coward

Selected Verses

1Kings 19:11-13	Jer. 31:10	1Cor. 4:18-21	1Thes. 2:6-7
Ps. 103:13-18	Eze. 34:11-16	Gal. 5:22-23	1Tim. 3:3
Prov. 12:18	Zec. 9:9	Gal. 6:1	1Tim. 6:11
Prov. 15:1	Matt. 11:28-30	Phil. 4:5	2Tim. 2:24-26
Prov. 25:15	Matt. 12:18-21	Col. 3:12	1Peter 3:4
Isa. 40:11	John 10:1-16	Col. 3:19-21	1Peter 3:15

Memory Verse

"Be completely humble and gentle;
be patient, bearing with one another in love."

Ephesians 4:2

Topic Introduction

Gentleness means that you care about another person (or other living thing) and that you want to show him that he is important. Gentle people are usually good listeners. They show interest and are not in a hurry. They care about the little things that might not seem to matter much. And they are not looking for ways to judge you. In weakness, we all could use some gentleness. But God is the ultimate example-- as long as we are honestly and openly trying, He is amazingly gentle through all our mistakes and confusion.

Is it comfortable to be around people who do not display gentleness?

Literary Examples

Literature
The Black Stallion, Walter Farley
Gentle Ben, Walt Morey
The Year of Miss Agnes, Kirkpatrick Hill

Poetry
"Hiawatha", Henry Wadsworth Longfellow
"Play with Me", Marie Hall Ets

Collections

The Moral Compass:
    "About Angels"
    "All the World is Sleeping"
    "The Boy Who Kissed His Mother"
    "The Story of the Small Caterpillar"

McGuffey's Third Eclectic Reader:
    "Bird Friends" (16)
    "Speak Gently" (43)

McGuffey's Fourth Eclectic Reader:
    "The Lion" (23)
    "Susie's Composition" (37)

McGuffey's Fifth Eclectic Reader:
    "The Gentle Hand" (3)

Thomas the Tank Engine series:
    "Pop Goes the Diesel"
            (Duck and the Diesel Engine)

Additional Discussion Topic

   ❖ Good Shepherd image of Christ

Topic Analysis

Literary Examples
All Creatures Great and Small, James Herriot
Hunchback of Notre Dame, Victor Hugo
Otto of the Silver Hand, Howard Pyle

Thought Provokers

- ❖ Small children and animals seem to be able to sense a gentle spirit far better than adults. Why is this?
- ❖ People usually respond to suffering in one of two ways: 1) they harden their hearts to insulate themselves from the pain, or 2) they accept the pain and agonize through it. What are the character effects of these two responses? Is a gentle spirit strong evidence of how one has responded to suffering or can gentleness be effectively nurtured without suffering?
- ❖ Gentleness is generally a good place to start in dealing with people-problems. But, especially when the offense is serious or we are in a position of authority, there needs to be a good deal of motivation underlying the gentleness. How can we be both gentle and firm? How can we remain gentle even when we must apply unpleasant discipline?
- ❖ Gentleness helps assure people so that they do not "put up their guard" so quickly. How might this be a much more powerful means of persuasion than other more aggressive methods? Give an example of a historical disaster that was or could have been saved by the gentle approach. Describe the projected alternative effects.
- ❖ Gentleness is often depicted as a quiet and meek, almost camouflaging, personality trait. But gentleness can take on several forms-- from playing devil's advocate to kind-hearted teasing, from non-violent tussling to just backing off-- provided that the truth and the other's dignity are both affirmed through it (directly or indirectly). Describe someone you know who is gentle without being stereotypically so.
- ❖ Tenderness is a key ingredient to intimate relationships. What are some practical ways this can be maintained, without feeling forced? Why is an artificial gentleness so offensive or disconcerting? What makes them completely different? (Alternatively, what makes a good romance story believable?)

Servant-hood

Working for the betterment of someone else;
Voluntarily helping to relieve another's burden

Synonyms: Service, Helpfulness

Antonyms/obstacles: selfishness, indifference, slavery, coercion

Imitation: pampering

Hesitation: Risk of being neglected or unappreciated

Selected Verses

Josh. 24:14–15	John 12:26	Rom. 15:2–3	Eph. 6:7
Mark 1:30–31	John 13:1–16	1Cor. 12:5	Phil. 2:4–7
Mark 9:33–35	Acts 2:44–46	1Cor. 16:15	Col. 3:24
Mark 10:42–45	Acts 4:32–35	Gal. 5:13	1Tim. 5:3–5
Luke 10:38–42	Rom. 12:4–8	Gal. 6:1–2	1Peter 4:10–11
Luke 12:35–37	Rom. 13:4	Eph. 4:12	

Memory Verse

"Carry each other's burdens,
and in this way you will fulfill the law of Christ."

Galatians 6:2

Topic Introduction

Those who embrace servant-hood volunteer to help for the sake of helping. A servant attends to the little details that make a big difference, one small step at a time. They are the ones who clean, repair, organize, cook, supply, beautify, nurture-- all the things that are barely noticed if they are done well. But Jesus says, "...whatever you did for one of the least of these brothers of mine, you did for me." (Matthew 25:40)-- So He Who sees all counts all. The little things do matter, however small, and especially so if they are done with care and gladness. After Jesus wrapped a towel around His waist to wash dirty feet, He told us: "you should do as I have done for you" (John 13:15).

How does serving each other help to make a group stronger than just its individuals?

Literary Examples

Literature

Rebecca of Sunnybrook Farm,

                    Kate Wiggin Douglas

The Secret Garden, Frances Hodgson Burnett

Short Stories

"Little Snow White", Grimm brothers

The Tale of Mrs. Tiggy-Winkle, Beatrix Potter

Collections

The Moral Compass:
    "Beautiful Hands"
    "The Brownies"
    "The Hill"
    "The Legend of Saint Christopher"
    "What Bradley Owed"
    "Your Mission"
    "Your Second Job"

Aesop:
    "The Hedge and the Vineyard"
    "The Thief and His Mother"

McGuffey's Third Eclectic Reader:
    "Lend a Hand" (6)
    "Beautiful Hands" (24)
    "Which Loved Best?" (58)

McGuffey's Fourth Eclectic Reader:
    "True Manliness" (14-15)

Thomas the Tank Engine series:
    "Devil's Back" (*Mountain Engines*)
    "Mind That Bike" (*Really Useful Engines*)

Additional Discussion Topic

❖ Role of church deacons

❖ Trade jobs or share all chores
❖ Pick up litter along your street

Topic Analysis

Literary Examples
1984, George Orwell
Animal Farm, George Orwell
"The Higher Abdication", O. Henry
Little Women, Louisa May Alcott
"A Service of Love", O. Henry
"The Third Ingredient", O. Henry
Uncle Tom's Cabin, Harriet Beecher Stowe

Thought Provokers

❖ Describe how a servant-leader would act differently than a dictator.
❖ Servant-hood can be mistaken as relieving someone's load entirely. When might this be appropriate and when might it not? How can you practically distinguish between carrying another's burden and shouldering his load, as implied in Galatians 6:2-5?
❖ How far should you be able to see the positive effects of your service? What if you always saw good things from them? What if you never saw any good results? How are we to use these signs to judge where we should continue serving?
❖ How is serving someone different from pleasing them? Though they are often the same, when are they different? What is the purpose behind each of these approaches?
❖ Service can easily over-run lives, especially for people whose occupations require it. So how can you discern when you are serving a real need and when you are just pampering a want or encouraging irresponsibility? Certainly the gracious thing to do is generally give others the benefit of the doubt, but at some point (if possible), achieving their independence should be the goal. Why is this so vital-- for both of you?
❖ In life, especially when in a position of authority, it is often our task to teach responsibility-- or at least require it of another (accountability). Yet we are to have the attitude of a servant. How are we to know when to do which? Or can they be done simultaneously?
❖ How is servant-hood almost universally a willingness to sacrifice?
❖ A disinclination to go beyond oneself, usually manifested as self-centeredness, places an individual in a very precarious position. Self-absorption— be it of physical health, ambition, beauty, or something else— often begins to spiral downwards to deep psychological problems and leads to a bad end. (Many addictions begin this way.) Find some Biblical or historical examples of this. Why is this so consistently the case? Who might you serve best by rousing them to join you in serving others?

❖ Service to others is sometimes used as a disguise for disobedience (or inattention) to God. This can actually result in handicapping the faith and responsibility of those you are trying to serve. Romans 12:1-2 suggests the antidote to this. What does it look like practically though?

❖ Find a way to intentionally serve in a new way this week.

Hospitality

Welcoming others

Antonyms/obstacles: unfriendliness, fear, shame, over-busyness

Imitation: flaunting, performing

Hesitation: Opens yourself to judgment

Selected Verses

Gen. 18:1-8	2Kings 6:18-23	Luke 24:13-32	1Tim. 5:9-10
Gen. 24:16-33	Matt. 10:40-42	Acts 28:7-10	Philem. 7
Josh. 2	Matt. 25:31-46	Rom 12:13	Philem. 22
Judg. 13:2-21	Luke 9:1-5	Rom. 16:23	Heb. 10:34
2Sam. 9	Luke 9:48	1Cor. 10:27-30	1Peter 4:9
1King 17:7-16	Luke 14:12-14	2Cor. 13:12	2John 10-11
2Kings 4:8-17	Luke 14:15-24	Gal. 4:13-15	3John 8

Memory Verse

"Do not forget to entertain strangers,
for by so doing
some people have entertained angels without knowing it."

Hebrews 13:2

Topic Introduction

Hospitality means that you do your best to make a person feel comfortable in an unfamiliar situation. You want to make them feel valued and accepted, but not awkward. Usually the best place to start is with a smile. (What else can you do to welcome others?) A hospitable person is not afraid to spend the best he has on his guests-- his time, thoughts, energy, skills, and resources-- to make certain they know that they are important just as they are. By practicing hospitality, we are reflecting the open arms of Jesus Christ and His warm-hearted invitation of "Come to Me" that He longs for every soul to accept.

How do people react to an inhospitable place?

Literary Examples

Literature
The House at Pooh Corner, A. A. Milne
Winnie-the-Pooh, A. A. Milne

Short Stories
May I Bring a Friend?,
                        Beatrice Schenk de Regniers
Mr. Gumpy's Motor Car, John Burningham
The Tale of Mr. Jeremy Fisher, Beatrix Potter
The Tale of Mrs. Tittlemouse, Beatrix Potter
Tawny Scrawny Lion, Kathryn Jackson

Collections

The Moral Compass:
    "Why the Evergreen Trees Never
                Lose Their Leaves"

McGuffey's Fifth Eclectic Reader:
    "The Righteous Never Forsaken" (25)

Thomas the Tank Engine series:
    "Little Old Twins" *(The Little Old Engine)*

Additional Discussion Topic

❖ Barnabas and Paul (Acts 9:26-30)

Activity Idea

❖ Host a meal for someone

Topic Analysis

Literary Examples
Blandings Castle series, P. G. Wodehouse
"Hostages to Momus", O. Henry
Invisible Man, Ralph Ellison

Thought Provokers

- ❖ Is hospitality only in the actual hosting or does it also include the invitation? You must be willing and prepared to give before you actually do. And surely, your invitation must itself be welcoming before anyone would be willing to accept it. What does this say about a personal invitation over a written one? Explain the difference.

- ❖ Hospitality seems to be one of those virtues that appears to be just a hodge-podge of other virtues. Which ones might it include?

- ❖ If fear is a great obstacle, the first step is to identify the specific fears. So what fears would hinder hospitality? How might they be overcome?

- ❖ Sometimes the volume of work involved in meeting certain expectations hinders us from practicing hospitality. Practically, what does hospitality include? Make a pie chart to represent the importance of each (including things such as a clean house/facility, tasteful decorations, food, friendly greetings). Does this help to dissolve some expectations, or can you host someone with simpler ones?

- ❖ Acceptance without unreasonable judgment or expectation is key to hospitality. But the proper degree of a welcoming spirit is also important in making someone feel significant and comfortable. Casual but genuine questions are one good approach in many situations. What are some good approaches to "breaking the ice" for you? How might you vary your approach depending on the response/attitude/personality of your guest?

- ❖ Hospitality is best learned in practice. Find a creative way to practice it this week.

Peace

Calmness in spirit and between hearts

Synonym: Calmness

Antonyms/obstacles: discord, anxiety, strife, worry, devisiveness

Imitations: comfort, conformity, making concessions

Hesitation: Compromises your ideal world

Selected Verses

Ps. 23	Prov. 17:27	Rom. 5:1-2	1Thes. 5:13
Ps. 46	Prov. 19:13	Rom. 12:16-18	1Tim. 2:1-2
Prov. 3:25-26	Prov. 21:9	Rom. 14:19-22a	2Tim. 2:23-24
Prov. 11:12	Prov. 26:20-21	Rom. 15:5-6	Titus 3:9
Prov. 12:20	Ecc. 10:14a	1Cor. 14:33a	James 3:18
Prov. 14:30	Matt. 5:9	2Cor. 13:11	1Peter 5:7
Prov. 16:28	Mark 9:50	Eph. 6:15	
Prov. 17:1	Luke 12:22-32	Phil. 4:6-7	
Prov. 17:14	John 14:27	Col. 3:15	

Memory Verse

"Be still, and know that I am God..."

Psalm 46:10a

Topic Introduction

Peace is the certainty of safety. Peace between people means that neither intends to harm the other. Even if there are some wounds, there is an openness to fix the problem or misunderstanding. Peace with God is knowing that He has you in His hands while you intend to choose what honors Him. Keeping peace means both people are trying. And when God and His promises are at one end, we really can have a peace through all sorts of trouble because He is stronger than all of them. Jesus says, "…in me you may have peace. In this world you will have trouble. But take heart! I have overcome the world" (John 16:33).

How does a group of people act when there is no peace?

Literary Examples

Literature
Caddie Woodlawn, Carol Ryrie Brinks
Homer Price, Robert McCloskey
Strawberry Girl, Lois Lenski

Short Stories
The Christmas Coat, Clyde Robert Bulla
The Story of Ferdinand, Munro Leaf

Hymns
"Be Thou My Vision", Mary Byrne
"It is Well with My Soul",
Horatio G. Spafford
"Rock of Ages, Cleft for Me",
Augustus Toplady
"When Peace, Like a River",
Horatio Spafford

Collections

The Book of Virtues:
  "Why Frog and Snake Never Play
Together"

The Moral Compass:
  "In the Uttermost Parts of the Sea"
  "My Two Homes"
  "One, Two, Three"
  "The Town Mouse and the Country
Mouse"

Aesop:
  "The Lion and the Goat"

McGuffey's Third Eclectic Reader:
  "The Echo" (33)
  "The Seven Sticks" (44)

McGuffey's Fourth Eclectic Reader:
  "Evening Hymn" (34)
  "The Winter King" (43)

Thomas the Tank Engine series:
  "Drip-Tank"
    (*More about Thomas the Tank Engine*)
  "Gordon Goes Foreign"
    (*The Eight Famous Engines*)
  "Steam-roller" (*Gallant Old Engine*)

- ❖ Fellowship
- ❖ Death

Activity Idea

- ❖ Play with a Chinese finger trap

Topic Analysis

Literary Examples
Pride and Prejudice, Jane Austen
"The Street That Got Mislaid", Patrick Waddlington
Three Men in a Boat, Jerome K. Jerome
War and Peace, Leo Tolstoy

Thought Provokers

- ❖ "Peace begins with open hearts." Make a "peace begins" quote too.
- ❖ What is the difference between peace and indifference? What is the difference between being at peace and being comfortable? In war (actual or metaphorical), how is having a truce different from being at peace?
- ❖ Can peace ever be one-sided? For example, if a man is very comfortable in his marriage and knows that his wife is looking out for his best interest, he certainly feels a certain degree of peace. However, in his comfort, he may become negligent and his wife no longer feels protected. Is this husband really at peace or is this just an instance of "ignorance is bliss"?
- ❖ Might we have peace about a situation without having peace within it? Describe an instance of this.
- ❖ There are people who hold (even unconsciously) to the creed of "peace at all costs". What are some things they might be sacrificing to follow this principle? How then do you know what to sacrifice for peace and what not to?
- ❖ It has been said that the best way to maintain peace in a hostile world is to maintain a strong defensive plan. Is this wise or really just a subtle attack against peace?
- ❖ Can there ever be peace between two people/groups without justice? How is satisfying each other's sense of justice key to peace?
- ❖ Peace is a difficult thing to restore once it has been broken, because trust has been violated. Can there be peace without trust, particularly in the period of rebuilding trust? Does this justify the need for laws, walls, and personal boundaries?

❖ There are certain degrees to peace. For example, people of different fundamental spiritual beliefs can never really have a deep peace between them. (For having a basis of appeal in a mutually agreed authority is essential to true peace and fellowship.) But finding compromise over more superficial disagreements is certainly feasible. What are these degrees and who has them?

❖ How is the idea of having an identity strongly connected to having peace? What is the nature of an identity which brings true peace within-- often then extending outwards?

❖ Jesus has some seemingly conflicting teachings and examples about peace. Find some. Is there any consistency to what He is telling us? What?

❖ Is it ever right to counter violence with violence? If so, what is the difference in motivations behind these two acts of violence? How do we know when the means justifies the end of achieving peace and when it does not?

Charity

Giving with the intent to help another without self-benefit or condition

Synonym: Alms-giving

Antonyms/obstacles: greed, selfishness, usury

Imitations: cheap charity, boom-a-rang giving

Hesitation: Unappreciated or wasted sacrifice

Selected Verses

Deut. 15:7-11	Matt. 5:40-42	Luke 12:33-34	James 1:27
Deut. 24:14-22	Matt. 6:1-4	Luke 18:18-25	James 2:15-17
Prov. 14:31	Matt. 7:12	Acts 10:1-8	James 3:16
Prov. 21:13	Matt. 10:42	Rom. 12:13	1John 3:17-18
Prov. 28:27	Matt. 25:31-46	1Cor. 10:24	
Prov. 31:8-9	Luke 3:7-11	Gal. 2:10	
Prov. 31:20	Luke 6:34-35	Phil. 2:4	

Memory Verse

""""I tell you the truth,
whatever you did for one of the least of these brothers of mine,
you did for me.""""

Matthew 25:40

Topic Introduction

Charity is all about giving to someone where we notice he has a need. A need is something a person must have to be healthy. It could be food, clean water, or shelter. (What are some other physical needs?) Or it could be education, skills, help, encouragement, or even a smile. We cannot help everyone, but we can all help someone somehow. Who do you know that could use something so that they could be stronger? What do you have that you could give to help that person?

What blessings do we miss when we do not practice charity?

Literary Examples

Literature
Robin Hood, any child's version
The Story of Doctor Dolittle, Hugh Lofting

Short Stories
A Fly Went By, Mike McClintock
"Medio Pollito", Hispanic folktale
The Story of a Fierce Bad Rabbit, Beatrix Potter
"Thumbelina", Hans Christian Andersen

Collections

The Moral Compass:
  "The Happy Prince"
  "Margaret of New Orleans"
  "Saint Catherine and the Silver Crucifix"
  "Saint Martin and the Beggar"
  "The Star Jewels"

McGuffey's Third Eclectic Reader:
  "The New Year" (27)
  "Mary's Dime" (64)
  "Mary Dow" (65)

McGuffey's Fourth Eclectic Reader:
  "Why the Sea is Salt" (3-4)

McGuffey's Fifth Eclectic Reader:
  "'I Pity Them'" (21)
  "The Tea Rose" (38)

Thomas the Tank Engine series:
  "Thomas and the Breakdown Train"
                    (*Thomas the Tank Engine*)

Additional Discussion Topics

❖ Rich Man and Lazarus (Luke 16:19-31)
❖ Legend of St. Nicholas
❖ Purpose of imaginary gift-givers (e.g. Santa Claus, Tooth-fairy)

Activity Idea

❖ Collect for a food pantry or other mission project

Topic Analysis

Literary Examples
"Christmas by Injunction", O. Henry
"The Discounters of Money", O. Henry
"The Garden Party", Katherine Mansfield
"Hygeia at the Solito", O. Henry
The Merry Adventures of Robin Hood, Howard Pyle
"The Renaissance at Charleroi", O. Henry
"Two Thanksgiving Day Gentlemen", O. Henry

Thought Provokers

- ❖ Compare and contrast charity and servant-hood.
- ❖ Much coddling is done in the name of charity. What is a good way to avoid this sort of thing?
- ❖ One modern idea of charity is really more of a giving out of convenience or a guiltless disposal. While intensely practical and good stewardship, how can considering it as a charitable work really end up stealing more dignity from another than it restores?
- ❖ In secular circles, charity can become quite an advertised virtue-- suggesting that if it is present, others are too. Can you have charity without integrity? Can you have charity without some degree of secrecy?
- ❖ Are all gifts given without obligation a form of charity? Why or why not?
- ❖ Is it right to give to someone who will most likely misuse the gift? Just not appreciate the gift? Invest it in something harmful? If we should, how are we to judge the motivations of others when we give? Should we attach conditions to it?
- ❖ Individually, charity is often given more as a transaction: where in turn we may expect wages, spiritual favor, honor, a gift in return, kudos, or something else to our benefit. Does this boomerang effect negate the virtue? How might the gift of this kind of "loaded giving" really become entirely despicable to the receiver? Does this suggest that true charity quite often *must* be bittersweet?
- ❖ What are some disadvantages (both to the giver and the receiver) when a gift is *not* given in secret? What are the advantages?
- ❖ Do secular charity/service programs really work? If so, which ones and why? In an imperfect world, while not closed to God, should not there be some services available that are separate from the "Christian" label and whatever stigma it might bring with it in people's minds? What do these effective charities have in common? So can true charity ever really be separated from the gospel?

Duty

Fulfilling self-directed obligations as the opportunity arises

Synonyms: Stewardship, Nobility

Antonyms/obstacles: neglect, wastefulness, debt, frivolity, impositions

Imitations: expectation juggling, gruelingly willful efforts

Hesitation: Risk that your efforts will be insignificant

Selected Verses

Gen 1:26–29	Ecc. 12:13	Luke 10:38–42	Gal. 6:10
Gen. 2:15	Isa. 19:21	Luke 17:7–10	Col. 4:1
2Sam. 11:7-13	Isa. 32:8	Luke 19:11–26	2Thes. 3:13
2Chr. 31:5	Mal. 3:8–12	Luke 20:21-25	1Tim. 3:13
Prov. 3:9–10	Matt. 17:24–27	Rom. 13:6–8	1Tim. 4:12–14
Prov. 3:27	Mark 12:13-17	2Cor. 9:6-7	2Tim. 4:5

Memory Verse

"Let no debt remain outstanding,
except the continuing debt to love one another…"

Romans 13:8

Topic Introduction

Duty is doing what you know you should do when you know you should do it. Sometimes that means brushing your pet or flossing your teeth. Sometimes it means picking up someone else's litter or saying "I'm sorry". Sometimes it means something even greater, depending on what the Holy Spirit is asking you. But duty is always yours. Your duties are not exactly the same as anyone else's, so while others can encourage you, they cannot make you do them willingly. You must see for yourself how they are good. That does not excuse us though, because we all have duties and God's best plan requires us to fulfill them ourselves.

Who suffers when people do not step up to do their duties?

Literary Examples

Literature
Redwall, Brian Jacques
The Voyage of the Dawn Treader, C. S. Lewis

Collections

The Book of Virtues:
  "Jack and the Beanstalk"
  "Paul Revere's Ride"

The Moral Compass:
  "Dr. Johnson and His Father"
  "God Will See"
  "The Gorgon's Head"
  "The Legend Beautiful"

McGuffey's Fourth Eclectic Reader:
  "Waste Not, Want Not" (21)

Thomas the Tank Engine series:
  "Stop Thief!" *(Really Useful Engines)*
  "Peter Sam and the Refreshment Lady"
                (Four Little Engines)
  "The Sad Story of Henry"
                (The Three Railway Engines)

Additional Discussion Topics

❖ Tithing
❖ Voting
❖ Conservation
❖ Simple living
❖ Making promises
❖ Good health habits
❖ Supporting good causes and not supporting bad causes
❖ Cultivating natural abilities (Parable of the Talents)

Topic Analysis

Literary Examples
Billy Budd, Herman Melville
"A Departmental Case", O. Henry
"The Guardian of the Accolade", O. Henry
Jeeves series, P. G. Wodehouse
"The Ransom of Mack", O. Henry
The Warden, Anthony Trollope
The Yearling, Marjorie Rawlings

Thought Provokers

- ❖ What are some examples in daily life of duties to be done? What would happen if they were *never* done? What would happen if they were done *too* religiously?

- ❖ We must sometimes give beyond our comfort, but not way beyond. What might happen if you do much more than is your duty? How do you know when you have come to allow your duties to dictate you rather than you dictating your duties? What is a good response to someone who is doing this?

- ❖ Duty is like perseverance, in that it keeps us going in the routine (though tiring or unpleasant). But sometimes duty is unconventional too. What is a Biblical example of someone whose duty was overridden by God's intervention? What do you think were the reactions of the people around them to their "failure to do their duty"?

- ❖ Duty might be thought of as how you invest your spare energies for the good of humanity. No one else can know how much you can give and still maintain a good balance in your life. Nor can they dictate what is valuable to you. So duties must be self-directed. What is a good response to someone asking you to do too much? How do you know where to draw the line?

- ❖ There are all sorts of people who are willing and anxious to tell us what our duties are: duties as sons or daughters, students, employees, citizens, Christians, friends, etc. How do we sort out which are right and which are not?

- ❖ How is duty different from responsibility? Why would people try to make them sound like the same thing? What might be an end result from clouding the distinction?

- ❖ "You cannot do everything, but you can do something." is a good phrase describing duty. (How is this similar to loyalty?) Your passions and strengths are good indicators of what "something" you would be most suited to do. What is yours? Where do you or could you apply it?

- ❖ As Christians, temptation very often arises as some duty-- often with virtuous appearances-- that we have over-and-above another one that does not really appear as important. Practically, how do we weigh the importance of one good thing over another? What are the signs that we have made a wrong choice? A right choice?

❖ Being our own caretakers can be an over-emphasized or an over-looked form of stewardship. Certainly we should "consider others better than [ourselves]" (Philippians 2:3) and "not worry about your life" (Matthew 6:25), but does that imply we should *not* make an effort to meet our own basic needs? Other verses however suggest that we should work hard to supply things for ourselves so that we will not be a burden to others. So how do we know when to halt our outside duties to focus on filling our own needs (body, mind, and spirit), without becoming selfish or self-indulgent? What exactly constituents a need anyway?

❖ Viewing our life and circumstances as a stewardship rather than a responsibility is often very freeing, in that we are not responsible for what we cannot control (though we are responsible for our behavior-- which is what we *can* control). What are the effects if we think we are responsible for our circumstances? What are the effects if we believe that the circumstances are God's responsibility?

Hope

Focus on the end good

Antonyms/obstacles: hopelessness, despair, depression, self-pity

Imitations: optimism, self-confidence

Hesitation: Risk in it proving to be futile

Selected Verses

Job 13:15a	Isa. 49:15–16	Rom. 15:13	Titus 1:2
Ps. 25:3	Jer. 29:11	1Cor. 13:13	Heb. 6:19
Ps. 42:5	Luke 12:32–34	2Cor. 1:8–10	Heb. 7:18–19
Ps. 62:5	John 14:2–3	2Cor. 4:18	Heb. 11:16
Ps. 147:11	Rom. 4:18	Col. 1:27–28	1Peter 1:3–4
Prov. 17:22	Rom. 5:4–5	Col 3:1–4	1Peter 1:13
Isa. 40:30–31	Rom. 8:24–25	1Thes. 5:8	1John 3:2–3

Memory Verse

"For this God is our God for ever and ever;
he will be our guide even to the end."

Psalm 48:14

Topic Introduction

Hope is knowing that God is perfectly good and that He is going to do what He promised to do. Whatever troubles we might have right now will all work out in the end for His good. It is what motivates us to keep going when things around us keep urging us to give up. Hope is like a faint light in an otherwise dark cavern. It is always reaching for something better. It is trying to peek into heaven. It is using our imaginations of what God's Word reveals to reach upward, even when our energy is spent. According to 1 Corinthians 13:13, it is one of the three most important and lasting virtues. Without hope, there would not be much reason to practice any of the others. (And if it is one of the eternal virtues, that means we will able to keep reaching for more of the wonder and mystery of God for all of eternity too!)

How can hope change a person?

Literary Examples

Literature
The Door in the Wall, Marguerite de Angeli
Pollyanna, Eleanor H. Porter
Velveteen Rabbit, Margery Williams

Picture Book
The Carrot Seed, Ruth Krauss

Poetry
"Hope is the Thing with Feathers",
                                    Emily Dickinson

Hymns
"Battle Hymn of the Republic",
                                    Julia Ward Howe
"Because He Lives", William Gaither
"Blessed Assurance", Fanny Crosby
"The Solid Rock", Edward Mote

Collections

McGuffey's Third Eclectic Reader:
    "We Are Seven" (63)

McGuffey's Fourth Eclectic Reader:
    "Jeannette and Jo" (22)

McGuffey's Fifth Eclectic Reader:
    "The Reaper and the Flowers" (28)
    "The Relief of Lucknow" (47)

Thomas the Tank Engine series:
    "Bluebells of England"
                    (*Stepney the "Bluebell" Engine*)
    "Toby and the Stout Gentleman"
                    (*Toby the Tram Engine*)

Activity Idea

❖ Plant a seed

Topic Analysis

Literary Examples
"Metamorphosis", Franz Kafka
The Robe, Lloyd C. Douglas
The Vicar of Wakefield, Oliver Goldsmith

Thought Provokers

- ❖ Hope is often used as a word expressing optimism-- where it may or may not come true. Biblical hope rests more a certainty of God's promise and character. Write a statement for each definition that helps highlight the difference.
- ❖ Make a list of as many of God's promises or His characteristics as you can. Keep this list as a reminder in a difficult time and see if it helps to restore hope.
- ❖ How is having hope different from having expectations? Christ's mission was basically one of restoring hope, but this required a great deal of time breaking down expectations. (See the book of Luke.) While similar, how can expectations hinder hope?
- ❖ Resilience is the ability to bounce back. Certainly despairing people are not resilient, but does this necessarily mean that it is a characteristic of hope? Might it have a different source-- if so, what?
- ❖ What role do we have in bringing hope to fruition?
- ❖ Hope is an often overlooked but key ingredient to prayer. We need to be expectant (without having expectations) of God's ability and willingness to address our *real* concerns. How might someone incorporate a more hopeful attitude into his prayer life?
- ❖ If hope is a good medicine (Proverbs 17:22), how might you help to give a glimmer of hope to someone who seems hopeless? Try it this week.
- ❖ How might hope be made stronger through extreme trial? How might it also be lost?
- ❖ Despair is a serious but prevalent problem in our society today. Though there are several asserted techniques for tackling it, there is really only one solution-- One that transcends the circumstances. What are some of these methods people (particularly non-Christians) use for abating despair, and how does each fall short of addressing reality?
- ❖ Do a Bible survey of heaven and list its characteristics. How is it really more than a mindless, surrealistic existence? What hope can this offer?

Wisdom

Objective understanding of what is best

Synonyms: Prudence, Discernment, Shrewdness

Antonyms/obstacles: foolishness, rashness, naivety, folly

Imitations: cleverness, cynicism

Hesitation: Risk in being dismissed or wrong

Selected Verses

Ps. 19:7	Prov. 15:33	Prov. 29:15	Eph. 5:15
Ps. 111:10	Prov. 16:16	Ecc. 9:17	Col. 2:3
Prov. 2:6	Prov. 19:8	Dan. 12:3	Col. 4:5
Prov. 10:13-14	Prov. 19:20	Matt. 7:6	1Thes. 5:21
Prov. 14:12	Prov. 21:30	Matt. 7:24-27	James 1:5
Prov. 14:15	Prov. 24:13-14	Rom. 11:33-34	James 3:13
Prov. 14:33	Prov. 28:26	1Cor. 1:17ff	James 3:17

Memory Verse

"'But wisdom is proved right by her actions.'"

Matthew 11:19b

Topic Introduction

Wisdom can spot the difference between what looks right and what is right. It understands the dangers and benefits of the different options and chooses what would be best. Wisdom usually sees a little more than usual: sometimes other possible choices, sometimes methods for uncovering true motivations, sometimes ways to clarify ideas or handle problems. Only the Holy Spirit sees perfectly and knows what is best, so that is the first place to look for it. The rest is developing the art of applying Godly principles well. And in the end, we will be able to see it for what it was because "wisdom is proved right by her actions" (Matthew 11:19).

What are the results of unwise decisions?

Literary Examples

Short Stories
"Henny-Penny" or "Chicken Little", folktale
Thidwick, the Big-Hearted Moose, Dr. Seuss
"The Three Little Pigs", traditional fable
"The Tiger, the Brahman, and the Jackal",
                                Indian folktale

Poetry
"If-", Rudyard Kipling
"Three Wise Men of Gotham",
                    The Real Mother Goose

Collections

The Moral Compass:
    "The Man Who Loved War Too Much"
    "The Fox and the Cat"
    "The Golden Tripod"
    "The Golden Windows"

Aesop:
    "The Boy Bathing"
    "The Miller, His Son, and Their Donkey"
    "The Two Frogs"

McGuffey's Third Eclectic Reader:
    "True Courage" (52)

McGuffey's Fifth Eclectic Reader:
    "The Blind Men and the Elephant" (96)

Thomas the Tank Engine series:
    "Danger Points" *(Mountain Engines)*
    "Leaves" *(Gordon the Big Engine)*

Additional Discussion Topics

- ❖ Solomon's judgment (1 Kings 3)
- ❖ Valuable pearl parable (Matthew 13:44-46)
- ❖ Tact

Topic Analysis

Literary Examples

Emma, Jane Austen
"The Lightning-Rod Man", Herman Melville
Richard II, William Shakespeare
Sense and Sensibility, Jane Austen

Thought Provokers

- ❖ What would be a good definition of wisdom? How does Godly wisdom differ from worldly wisdom?

- ❖ Scripture associates humility closely with wisdom, both as a cause and as an effect. Find three such verses.

- ❖ Much of sorting out what is wise boils down to determining spiritually which are causes and which are effects. For example, one may argue that if you go to church, then you are right with God; when really it is more true that if you are right with God, then you will go to church. Find two examples of this sort of confusion from every-day life. How does this insight help clear up the true situation?

- ❖ Sometimes as Christians, we are tempted to sacrifice much for what appears to be the greater good-- and indeed we ought to. But where should choosing what is safe (if even only for ourselves) supersede upholding some other virtue? Find a Biblical example of someone who chose rightly to be safe over some other duty. Find an example of someone who chose to sacrifice their safety for their duty.

- ❖ There are many people who try to sound wise by being shrew in their arguments, or good at rhetoric. While this skill may be very useful in some instances, it is not something in which Jesus would engage the Pharisees for very long. Perhaps this is because very often rhetoric is just a shell to guard some secret justification for a deeper desire. What is a good way to cut through this "wisdom of this age" to the heart of the matter?

- ❖ Much of wisdom has to do with seeing clearly, beyond pretenses and justifications. (So in some ways, we should ask not so much what Jesus would do as what Jesus would see.) So how can we do that in a world that is so good at "wearing the mask" and putting up a bold front? Should taking a risk at identifying reality be a marked characteristic of Christians, especially considering that it is essential to witnessing? But how can we do this well-- without being arbitrary?

- ❖ "[W]isdom is proven right by her actions" (Matthew 11:19). If the "proof" is that it works out in the end in the inner most being, how long must we wait to distinguish if obstacles are just set-backs or are serious judgment problems (i.e., folly)? How can you be sure that you are traveling on the right road in the midst of the journey?

Faithfulness

Staying true to a commitment

Synonym: Fidelity

Antonyms/obstacles: unfaithfulness, infidelity, divorce, swearing

Imitations: minimalism, technical adherence

Hesitation: Limits your options

Selected Verses

Gen. 17:9-11	Ps. 15:4b	Prov. 20:6	Lam. 3:22-33
Gen. 42:33-37	Ps. 50:14	Prov. 20:25	Jonah 2:9
Lev. 5:4	Ps. 73:12-17	Prov. 25:19	Matt. 5:33-37
Num. 30:2-5	Ps. 111:5-9	Prov. 28:20	Rom. 12:12
Deut. 23:21-23	Prov. 3:3-4	Ecc. 5:4-7	Gal. 5:25
1Sam. 1:1-28	Prov. 14:14	Isa. 54:5-10	James 5:12
1Kings 8:56	Prov. 16:6	Jer. 3:8-11	1Peter 4:10

Memory Verse

"'Be faithful, even to the point of death,
and I will give you the crown of life.'"

Revelation 2:10b

Topic Introduction

Faithfulness means keeping your promise, even when it is not working out well. If we are to reflect what God is like, we need to show that His promises do not change-- by being faithful to our own. Our words matter to the people around us, so we need to carefully consider when we speak and what we say. "…[O]ut of the overflow of [the] heart, [the] mouth speaks" (Luke 6:45), so if our hearts are full of Jesus, the words of our mouths must be like a rock. No excuses allowed.

What would it be like to work with an unfaithful person?

Literary Examples

Literature
Charlotte's Web, E. B. White

Short Stories
"The Frog-King", Grimm brothers
Horton Hatches an Egg, Dr. Seuss

Hymns
"Great is Thy Faithfulness",
                                    Thomas Chisholm
"O Come All Ye Faithful", traditional hymn

Poetry
"Paul Revere's Ride",
                        Henry Wadsworth Longfellow

Collections

Aesop:
   "The Wolf and the Crane"

McGuffey's Fourth Eclectic Reader:
   "Dare to Do Right" (67-68)

McGuffey's Fifth Eclectic Reader:
   "Respect for the Sabbath Rewarded" (13)

Thomas the Tank Engine series:
         "Bertie's Chase" *(Edward the Blue Engine)*
         "Old Faithful" *(Four Little Engines)*
         "Percy's Promise" *(Percy the Small Engine)*

Additional Discussion Topics

- ❖ Keeping your promises
- ❖ Value of the spoken word
- ❖ Covenants
- ❖ Infallibility of God's promises

Topic Analysis

Literary and Dramatic Examples
Fidelio, Ludwig van Beethoven (an opera)
Lady Windermere's Fan, Oscar Wilde
The Little Nugget, P. G. Wodehouse

Thought Provokers

❖ How are faithfulness and trustworthiness alike? How are they different?

❖ Faithfulness is one of those virtues that is displayed most in the daily grind of life, through the small decisions. As such, it is usually through these small things that others will judge your faithfulness-- and probably rightly so. What are some particular examples of faithfulness in the daily lives of the people around you?

❖ We are obligated to be faithful to our word, so we should somberly weigh the promises we make (or even the expectations we raise) when we speak. Even though we cannot predict the future, we need to strive to be faithful in everything. But how far should we expect and require others to be faithful? Does it matter whether they profess to be Christians or not?

❖ One of the gravest dangers to faithfulness is impulse. What we decide is right in a moment of peace may not look so attractive in the midst of a trial, and the old promises are quickly amended with excuses and exceptions... While humanly understandable and forgivable, they are usually nevertheless shameful. This is clearer if we imagine hearing them rather than making them. Make a list of eight common excuses you make or hear. What is being compromised in each?

❖ There is a certain hierarchy to faithfulness, in that we should be more faithful to God and our family than, say, to our co-workers. While you should not lightly break your word, there are times you must be more faithful to one promise than to another, which happen to contradict. Make a hierarchy of faithfulness chart for yourself.

❖ There are times when our faithfulness will be sorely tested by long and seemingly unnecessary trials. Regret and disgust at being used unjustly, misunderstood, or deceived are inevitable. Who is someone who was faithful to the full extent of his abilities, despite the reasonable or baleful opposition from inside and out? What were some of the results of his life?

❖ If we make a hasty promise which turns out to promote some evil, are we still obligated to be faithful to it? Give an example to support you opinion.

❖ How far are we obligated to promises that others have made in our name? Is it right to make promises for others, particularly for underlings? Is passive acquiescence to these vows others have made for us necessarily an agreement to and an acceptance of them?

❖ Sometimes with promises, there may come implications which we do not completely understand. Some of them may be legitimate and some of them may be just spurious obligation. How can you objectively judge what follows fairly from your promises and what does not? If this can quickly be reduced to legalism, is it really worth making any promises at all?

❖ Faithfulness to our convictions (with confession) is key to integrity. But our convictions must be consistent. One of the best ways to show (respectfully) the inconsistency of other world views is to show that if you are faithful to them, then you become inconsistent. Find an example of this.

Thoughtfulness

Viewing the situation through another's perspective and acting in response to it

Synonyms: Consideration, Graciousness, Gallantry

Antonyms/obstacles: thoughtlessness, inconsideration, apathy, contempt, disregard, criticism, favoritism, self-centeredness

Imitations: sentimentality, presumption, hyper-sensitivity

Hesitation: Risk of wasted efforts

Selected Verses

Ps. 41:1-3	John 1:35-45	Rom. 14:1-18	Heb. 10:24
Prov. 18:1	John 7:21-24	Rom. 15:1-3	Heb. 13:3
Prov. 18:16	John 11:17-37	Eph. 4:29	James 1:19
Jer. 38:1-13	Acts 9:36-39	Phil. 2:3-4	James 2:1-4
Dan. 1:3-16	Rom. 2:1-4	1Tim. 5:10	James 3:14-17
Luke 1:39-56	Rom. 12:15	Titus 3:1-2	1Peter 3:7

Memory Verse

"'Stop judging by mere appearance,
and make a right judgment.'"

John 7:24

Topic Introduction

Thoughtfulness is thinking like another person and trying to figure out what would be best for him instead of trying to only get what is best for you. It is a gift, a kindness, a word, or a service that is tailored to fit one particular person. It is the seal that glues friendship together because it shows that you have noticed what makes that person different and that you accept him exactly that way. We can be thoughtful of strangers too though, for nearly everyone craves a friendly nod or an encouraging word. But thoughtfulness is always about lifting the other person up and showing him that he is unique and important.

What does it feel like to overhear a thoughtless comment about you?

Literary Examples

<u>Short Stories</u>
Mr. Putter and Tabby series, Cynthia Rylant
Pierre, Mercer Mayer
"The Quiet Little Woman",
                    Louisa May Alcott
"Twelve Days of Christmas", Jack Kent

<u>Hymn</u>
"Moment by Moment", Daniel W. Whittle

Collections

The Book of Virtues:
    "Rocking Horse Land"

The Moral Compass:
    "Greedy"
    "Prince Harweda and the Magic Prison"

Aesop:
    "The Ant and then Dove"
    "The [Donkey's] Shadow"
    "The Fox and the Bramble"
    "The Horse and the Laden [Donkey]"

McGuffey's Third Eclectic Reader:
    "Susie and Rover" (67)

McGuffey's Fourth Eclectic Reader:
    "Two Ways of Telling a Story" (19)
    "Somebody's Darling" (55)

McGuffey's Fifth Eclectic Reader:
    "It Snows" (12)

Thomas the Tank Engine series:
    "Break Van" (*The Twin Engines*)
    "Bucking Bronco" (*Very Old Engines*)
    "Cows!" (*Edward the Blue Engine*)
    "Domeless Engines"
                (*Duck and the Diesel Engine*)
    "Edward and Gordon"
                (*The Three Railway Engines*)
    "James and the Bootlace"
                (*James the Red Engine*)
    "Mrs. Kyndley's Christmas"
                (*Toby the Tram Engine*)
    "Percy Runs Away" (*Troublesome Engines*)
    "Thomas, Percy and the Coal"
                (*More About Thomas the Tank Engine*)
    "Tit for Tat" (*Small Railway Engines*)

> ❖ Gift-giving

Topic Analysis

Literary and Dramatic Examples
Beowulf, Anonymous
"By Courier", O. Henry
"Cupid a la Carte", O. Henry
A Doll's House, Henrik Ibsen
"The Fiddler", Herman Melville
Meistersinger, Richard Wagner (an opera)
"The Missing Chord", O. Henry

Thought Provokers

> ❖ Thoughtfulness seems to permeate nearly every one-on-one contact, reflected in our conversation and behavior. What impressions does a thoughtful person leave in contrast to a self-centered one? List some adjectives that someone might use to describe each after a meeting with them.

> ❖ Thoughtfulness is especially obvious in gift-giving, for there is a big difference between an apt gift and a tasteless one. Where gift-giving can become such an obligation, how can we turn it into an opportunity for honoring another more with our thoughtfulness than with our extravagances? What might be some alternatives to traditional, tangible presents?

> ❖ Genuinely listening to another (and engaging them with questions) is probably one of the most identifying characteristics of thoughtfulness. While this does not mean that we must be entirely open-minded, it does mean giving the other a generous benefit of the doubt-- not as an end necessarily, but as a beginning of deeper discussions. Who is it that you might engage in this way?

> ❖ We are called to "bear with the failings of the weak" (Romans 15:1), yet also to"[hate] even the clothing stained by corrupted flesh" (Jude 23). Our response then depends on whether the individual is struggling with a mere weakness or a dangerous error. How are we to distinguish between the two, thereby determining how we are to respond?

> ❖ Habitual thoughtlessness is a difficult thing to confront in another. Usually the symptoms are subtle and varied, the person is generally completely ignorant of any problem, and confronting them places us in a dangerously hypocritical position. What is an appropriate way of dealing with occasional thoughtlessness to you? To others? What is an appropriate way of dealing with chronic thoughtlessness? To you? To others? What can we do to ensure that we do not become habitually thoughtless too?

> ❖ It is possible to become overly sensitive to others, being aware of and catering to their most subtle changes. While this might be appropriate at times, what is being compromised by inordinate attention? How might this be mistaken as being thoughtful?

❖ There are certain, often desperate, situations where a person cannot escape from their harmful predicament alone (e.g., drug addiction, slavery). Often the mere shame of this keeps them from seeking help; at other times, they may not even recognize that they *are* in a harmful predicament. While certainly God can rescue them Himself, might He also require your thoughtfulness to restore a person's life? Where have you noticed something that did not seem "quite right"? What can you do to respectfully investigate it further?

Honor

Upholding goodness in others with outward recognition

Synonyms: Blessing, Appreciation, Praise

Antonyms/obstacles: dishonor, disgrace, slander, fawning

Imitations: flattery, idolatry

Hesitation: Risk in affirming bad motivations

Selected Verses

Ex. 20:12	Prov. 22:1	Ecc. 7:1a	Gal. 1:10
Ps. 19:1–4a	Prov. 22:11	Matt. 5:14–16	Phil. 2:25–30
Ps. 146–150	Prov. 25:9–10	Matt. 7:15–20	2Tim. 2:15
Prov. 3:27	Prov. 25:27	Matt. 13:53–58	1Peter 2:17
Prov. 12:4	Prov. 27:21	Matt. 15:1–9	
Prov. 13:18	Prov. 29:23	1Cor. 10:31	
Prov. 20:11	Prov. 31:10–31	1Cor. 16:17–18	

Memory Verse

"Let everything that has breath praise the LORD.
Praise the LORD."

Psalm 150:6

Topic Introduction

Honor means that you somehow show someone that what he did was important and good. It means that we are not only supporting the person but also the work that he has done. The world even recognizes the importance of this virtue, in that they will frequently honor those who have accomplished something very important. It helps us to understand what greatness looks like. But within our own small worlds, we need to especially honor those who have given of their best for us, too. The invisible sacrifice is often more important than the visible. And Who has done the most for us and deserves the greatest honor we can find, with all our hearts and at every turn?

Without some sort of honor, how could we learn the difference between good and bad?

Literary Examples

Literature
The Horse and His Boy, C. S. Lewis

Short Stories
The Tale of Squirrel Nutkin, Beatrix Potter
"Toomai of the Elephants", *Jungle Book*,
Rudyard Kipling

Hymns

"All Glory, Laud and Honor", John Neale

"All Hail the Power of Jesus' Name",
Edward Perronet

"Crown Him with Many Crowns",
Matthew Bridges

"Fairest Lord Jesus", Joseph Seiss

"Holy, Holy, Holy! Lord God Almighty",
Reginald Heber

"How Great Thou Art",
Carl Boberg and Stuart Hine

"Immortal, Invisible", Walter Chalmers Smith

"O For a Thousand Tongues", Charles Wesley

"O Worship the King", Sir Robert Grant

"Praise God, from Whom All Blessings Flow",
Thomas Ken

"Praise to the Lord, the Almighty",
Joachim Neander

"To God Be the Glory", Fanny Crosby

Collections

The Moral Compass:
    "The Boy and the Angel"
    "How the Wise Man Found the King"

Aesop:
    "The Boasting Traveler"

McGuffey's Fourth Eclectic Reader:
    "The Creator" (46)

McGuffey's Fifth Eclectic Reader:
    "The Maniac" (9)

Thomas the Tank Engine series:
    "Bowled Out"
        (*Stepney the "Bluebell" Engine*)
    "Duck and Dukes" (*Very Old Engines*)
    "Paint Pots and Queens"
        (*Gordon the Big Engine*)
    "Toad Stands By"
        (*Oliver the Western Engine*)

❖ A.C.T.S. acronym of prayer (**A**doration-**C**onfession-**T**hanksgiving-**S**upplication)
❖ Worship

Activity Ideas

❖ List or act out expressions of honor
❖ Listen to hymns or praise songs

Topic Analysis

Literary Examples

"The Brief Debut of Tildy", O. Henry
Don Quixote de la Mancha, Miguel de Cervantes
"The Emancipation of Billy", O. Henry
"The Pendulum", O. Henry

Thought Provokers

❖ How is honor often related to respect? How can it be separate? (How can we show honor to someone even if we do not respect or if we possibly distrust the individual?)
❖ How can we honor someone (even God) when we have no natural desire to do so? What sorts of behaviors do you curb because you are honoring someone even if you instinctively know they deserve something quite different? Is this behavior unjust, insincere, or unwise then?
❖ There are often two opposite reactions to receiving an honor: a humble acceptance which spurs one onto greater things or a self-satisfied arrogance which dwells upon the accomplishment. Certainly we should give praise where it is due, but how can we temper the temptation towards pride in how we present an honor? And should we?
❖ Praise can be a powerful force, akin to encouragement, if given at the proper time. What might praising someone *before* there is any certainty of a positive outcome do for a struggling individual? Is this just giving them a false hope or is it a cheer of loyalty?
❖ Praising God in the midst of a difficulty-- in confidence of His provision though the details are desperately uncertain-- is a powerful faith-booster. What might it do for us if we praise God *before* we are certain of a "happy ending"? Find a Biblical example of "pre-earned" praise of God and its powerful results.
❖ In what ways is sin a dishonoring of God? Thinking of sin this way can often help us identify some areas of sinfulness that we habitually overlook. Is there an area like that for you? (But be wary too, because what one person does to honor God might be dishonorable for you to do and vice versa. So we really cannot judge others in unclear matters.)

- ❖ What is the difference between genuine praise and flattery? What is the difference between praise and boasting? How can we steer clear of these negative forms?
- ❖ Wonder is a key ingredient to motivating us to honor and giving us direction as to whom to honor. If we take the awe out of our praise, it often becomes flat and insincere. So how far should we go to try to understand and explain people and things if it will deflate the wonder of them (often leading to pride)? Do we run this risk with God?
- ❖ Adoration and worship are forms of honor that should be reserved for the three Persons of the Trinity. How does this look different than the honor of another person? List the contrasts. How is this difference made obvious to those who are observing us?
- ❖ Write a psalm or hymn.

Vigilance

Alert to attacks against goodness or to subtle gifts of goodness

Synonym: Watchfulness

Antonyms/obstacles: inattention, permissiveness, complacency, worldliness, resignation, slovenliness, ignorance

Imitations: suspicion, harshness, condemnation

Hesitation: Risk in causing offense

Selected Verses

Deut. 4:9	Hab. 2:1	Acts 20:28-31	1Tim. 4:16
Prov. 4:13	Zep. 1:12	Rom. 16:17-18	1Tim. 6:20-21
Prov. 4:23	Matt. 4:1-11	1Cor. 16:13	2Tim. 1:14
Prov. 7:2	Matt. 10:16-17a	2Cor. 11:4, 13-20	Heb. 2:1
Prov. 8:34	Matt. 16:6-12	Eph. 4:27	James 1:27
Prov. 13:24	Matt. 25:1-13	Eph. 5:6-13	James 4:7b
Prov. 16:17	Matt. 26:40-41	Col. 4:2	2Peter 3:16-17
Eze. 3:17	Mark 13:32-37	1Thes. 5:6	Rev. 3:2
Amos 6:1	Luke 12:15	1Thes. 5:21-22	Rev. 16:15
Micah 7:7	Luke 12:35-46	2Thes. 2:3	

Memory Verse

"Be self-controlled and alert.
Your enemy the devil prowls around like a roaring lion
looking for someone to devour."

1 Peter 5:8-9

Topic Introduction

Vigilance is watching out. It means we must think things through before we accept them. The world is full of dangers and deceptions of all kinds, many of which look innocent or good at the start. Satan specializes in trickery and illusions, and they are very convincing, especially if we are not watching out for them. But before we can watch out for attacks against love and truth, we have to know how to recognize the difference. The Scripture and Holy Spirit are the best guides, so get in the Word and on your knees often. Vigilance can also mean watching out for blessings too. God often appears in a still, small voice which is very easy to overlook. If we do not keep our hearts in tune, we can easily miss Him in so many, many ways.

What will happen if Satan evades our vigilance and takes a foothold?

Literary Examples

Literature
Henry and Ribsy, Beverly Cleary
The Silver Chair, C. S. Lewis
The Wizard of Oz, L. Frank Baum

Hymn
"Onward, Christian Soldiers",
Sabine Baring-Gould

Short Stories
"Hansel and Gretel", Grimm brothers
"The Pied Piper of Hamelin",
Grimm brothers
"Sleeping Beauty", Grimm brothers
The Tale of Jemima Puddle-Duck, Beatrix Potter

Collections

The Moral Compass:
  "The Camel's Nose"

Aesop:
  "The One-Eyed Doe"
  "The Sick Lion"
  "The Swallow's Advice"
  "The Trumpeter Taken Prisoner"
  "The Wild Boar and the Fox"

McGuffey's Third Eclectic Reader:
  "The Soldier" (32)
  "The Alarm Clock" (50)
  "Holding the Fort" (77)

Thomas the Tank Engine series:
  "Percy's Predicament" (*Branch Line Engines*)
  "Thomas and the Trucks"
    (*Thomas the Tank Engine*)

- ❖ Nehemiah (Nehemiah 4)
- ❖ World views
- ❖ Importance of critical thinking

Activity Ideas

- ❖ Play a "Simon Says" variation
- ❖ Make candy, pudding, grilled cheese, or anything else that requires careful watching

Topic Analysis

Literary Examples
The Screwtape Letters, C.S. Lewis
The 39 Steps, John Buchan

Thought Provokers

- ❖ Vigilance as a virtue is hardly emphasized at all in our society. How might this be a shrewd move on Satan's part?
- ❖ How is suspicion different from vigilance? Certainly we should be suspicious of certain things, but what and when?
- ❖ When you find yourself in a difficult situation, a moral dilemma often arises between being content (or patient, submissive, or respectful) and being vigilant and shrewd. (And it seems we each have a tendency to favor one side over the other in a majority of situations.) Once we have identified the problem, how then do we determine whether to fight (overtly or covertly), flee, or surrender/tolerate it? What are some Biblical principles and verses on deciding which to do, depending on the situation?
- ❖ Hidden motives, unspoken premises, and subtle obligations are quite common in our world. Often they are even disguised as virtues (i.e., receiving a gift from someone and then being expected to do something in return, particularly if it is something you would not normally give freely). How can we recognize and interrupt being deceived by this?
- ❖ God sent Nehemiah to build up the walls of Jerusalem (note though that there were gates also). Similarly, setting our own boundaries is a good application of vigilance. What sorts of boundaries do we need physically? Emotionally? Psychologically? Spiritually? Against what do they protect us?
- ❖ The principle of "turning the other cheek" and "not [resisting] an evil person" (Matthew 5:39-42) can be confusing in the light of vigilance. If vigilance is largely resistance, what exactly are we to resist and what are we not? What sort of ill treatment did Jesus accept? What behavior did He confront with harsh words? Are we to follow accordingly?

- ❖ Being vigilant requires us to make judgments. Biblical teaching on judging can be confusing however. What are we called to judge and not to judge? How does this help clarify where we need to be vigilant and where we should be diplomatic?
- ❖ Jesus' treatment of the Pharisees seems particularly harsh and almost unloving. But how is this application of vigilance really the most loving thing He could have done for them? How might this principle apply to us today?
- ❖ Evil is evil is evil. What are its tell-tale characteristics? List them. (To begin: Its purpose is to completely destroy. It masquerades as something innocent at first.) Then avoid them completely!!! (1 Thessalonians 5:22)

Earnestness

Doing intensely with pure and true motivations

Synonyms: Sincerity, Zealousness, Passion, Genuineness

Antonyms/obstacles: insincerity, sloppiness, hypocrisy, mediocrity, superficiality

Imitations: excitement, ambition, obsession, anxiety

Hesitation: Risk of making conspicuous mistakes

Selected Verses

Num. 25:10-13	Prov. 23:17	Mark 2:1-5	2Cor. 9:2
Deut. 4:29	Prov. 26:18-19	John 1:43-49	Gal. 4:18
1Sam. 16:7	Ecc. 6:11	John 2:13-17	Eph. 6:5-8
1Kings 19:19-21	Ecc. 9:10a	John 4:23-24	Phil. 1:9-10
1Chron. 28:9-10	Jer. 29:13	Rom. 10:1-3	1Thes. 2:3-9
2 Chron. 16:9a	Matt. 10:37-38	Rom. 12:9-11	1Thes. 5:19
Prov. 4:23	Matt. 13:44-46	2Cor. 1:12	Titus 2:14
Prov. 15:4	Matt. 23:26	2Cor. 2:17	
Prov. 19:2	Matt. 26:6-13	2Cor. 7:11-13	

Memory Verse

"Whatever you do,
work at it with all your heart,
as working for the Lord, not for men..."

Colossians 3:23

Topic Introduction

Earnestness means that you *really* want something, you show that it is important to you, and it almost does not matter what it costs you. When Jesus turned over the money changers' tables (Matthew 21:12-13), He really wanted a place for people to pray, and He was willing to make a mess and anger as many people as necessary to get it. But earnestness must reflect God's heart too. If we are willing to sacrifice so much, then we must be certain it is for the right cause and in the right way!

Is there any great historical figure who did *not* pursue his goal with earnestness?

Literary Examples

Literature   Short Stories
The Cay, Theodore Taylor   *Stop that Ball*, Mike McClintock
                                        "The White Seal", *Jungle Book*,
                                                                    Rudyard Kipling

Collections

The Moral Compass: *McGuffey's Fourth Eclectic Reader:*
   "All God's Creatures Have Work to Do"   "Good Will" (57)
   "For You and Me"
                                        Thomas the Tank Engine series:
Aesop: "A Close Shave" *(Duck and the Diesel Engine)*
   "The [Donkey] in the Lion's Skin"
   "The Fox and the Woodman"
   "The Hen and the Fox"
   "The Horse and the Groom"

Topic Analysis

Literary and Dramatic Examples
"The Defeat of the City", O. Henry
The Importance of Being Earnest, Oscar Wilde
L'Elisir D'Amore, Gaetano Donizetti (an opera)
"The Romance of a Busy Broker", O. Henry
"Shoes", O. Henry
Swan Lake, Pyotr Ilyich Tchaikovsky (a ballet)

❖ Zeal is a great motivator to accomplish big things, but it can also be directed to doing much harm (i.e., Muslim extremists, Saul's persecution of the Christians). How can we be sure that we are being zealous for the right things? Is this check something that should be done once or continually?

❖ Most people have a particular "passion" that is usually based on some intense experience or struggle they have had that they, in turn, hope to help others overcome. How should we respond to others' passions, even if we do not sympathize with them? What if we strongly disagree with them?

❖ Certainly there are some tasks we do that are perfunctory. Does not engaging our emotions in them necessarily mean that we are not earnest about them? Or does doing them despite our lack of enthusiasm exemplify our earnestness?

❖ What are the differences between ambition, obsession, passion, and zeal? How can we clarify the motivations in ourselves? In others?

❖ Oftentimes, our earnestness to see some good accomplished will manifest itself as anxiety-- we want *so* much to see something happen that we get bogged down by the details and our responsibilities in them. We can begin to compromise other things of value, like respect or peace or gentleness, to achieve the goal. Almost paradoxically, quiet trust (though not necessarily quiet voices or inaction) is the wiser choice. Describe a historical or personal situation where this has been illustrated.

❖ With zeal, we invest our mind, will, and energies to a large extent. But where one area increases, another area must be depleted (even if only temporarily). What areas are you willing to neglect (or have neglected) a little to invest more into your passion or calling?

❖ Though true of most virtues, sincerity especially requires the freedom not to act at all. What inevitably is the result of depleting this freedom-- both to the "task-master" and to his "slave"?

❖ One of the truest tests of sincerity is that it is spontaneous. How might that be used to test the earnestness of someone's claim?

❖ Another test of sincerity is opposition, especially from someone whom you consider "respectable." How ought we respond in such a situation? How might opposition also serve to strengthen earnestness?

❖ There are several other tests for sincerity which help distinguish it from excitement. List a few.

Submission

Attitude of yielding to the decisions or needs of another in good conscience

Synonyms: Deference, Acceptance

Antonyms/obstacles: quarrelsomeness, arguing, resistance, stubbornness, contentiousness

Imitations: automatic compliance, subservience

Hesitation: Risk of being used

Selected Verses

Job 36:15-16	Matt. 16:24-26	Phil. 2:14-15	James 4:6-7a
Job 37:19-23	Luke 1:38	Col. 3:18	James 4:6-7a
Prov. 13:13	Rom. 6:13	Titus 2:9-10	1Peter 2:13-18
Prov. 19:20	Rom. 10:3	Titus 3:1	1Peter 3:1-6
Prov. 29:1	Rom. 13:1-5	Heb. 12:9	
Matt. 10:37-39	1Cor. 16:15-16	Heb. 13:17	
Matt. 11:20-30	Eph. 5:21-24	James 1:21	

Memory Verse

"'Father, if you are willing,
take this cup from me;
yet not my will, but yours be done."

Luke 22:42

Topic Introduction

Submission is a willingness to allow another person to be in charge for a while. It can be like a yield sign on the road-- you sometimes need to let other people go first so that traffic will run smoothly for everyone. Sometimes there is no one who needs to go first, and sometimes it is your turn-- but it is always for the best of everybody, so we all can get where we are going. We need to submit to each other so that there is some order and equality, honoring God by working smoothly together for a common good. Submission can also be like carrying a load. If we spend all our time and energy trying to remove a burden that will not come off, we are easily worn out. If instead we accept the burden and keep trying, then we often find we are stronger in the end. This is the kind of submission God often asks of His people.

What would happen in a group if no one was willing to submit to anyone else?

Literary Examples

Short Stories
"Cinderella", European folktale
The Courage of Sarah Noble, Alice Dalgliesh

Hymns
"Have Thine Own Way, Lord!",
Adelaide Pollard
"Take My Life and Let It Be",
Frances Havergal

Collections

The Moral Compass:
   "Beethoven's Triumph"
   "On His Blindness"
   "Surrender at Appomattox"

Aesop:
   "The [Donkey] and His Driver"
   "The Oak and the Reed"

McGuffey's Fifth Eclectic Reader:
   "Little Victories" (101)

Thomas the Tank Engine series:
   "Crosspatch" (*Very Old Engines*)
   "Thomas in Trouble"
                    (*Toby the Tram Engine*)
   "Thomas, Terence, and the Snow"
              (*Tank Engine Thomas Again*)

Additional Discussion Topics

❖ Abraham and Sarah (Genesis 12-23)
❖ Esther (Esther 1-9)
❖ Bullying
❖ Surrendering

Activity Ideas

❖ Lead a blind-folded child
❖ Draw a picture by moving someone else's hand that is holding the pencil
❖ Play "Follow the Leader"

Topic Analysis

Literary Examples

Cheaper by the Dozen, Frank Gilbreath and Ernestine Carey

"Hearts and Crosses", O. Henry

Taming of the Shrew, William Shakespeare

Thought Provokers

❖ In your own words, how is submission different from obedience? How might it look the same?

❖ Submission is often thought of as an unthinking, unconditional acquiescence to another human authority above your conscience; almost as if you can submit better if you can disengage your heart, mind, and will-- giving someone else leave to redefine your identity. (Essentially this places another person in the dangerous position of being your liaison to God: a deadly practice! See Luke 16:13.) What Biblical principles temper this perspective of submission?

❖ What understanding must be in place between you and the one to whom you are submitting? What must be done if this influence proves to be inconsistent with Scripture or the Holy Spirit?

❖ Even if we are in a subordinate position, we must not submit to doing or enabling wrong-- which is different from submitting to the wrong behavior of others. We have control over ourselves but not over them. How can this be done well? Where does passive resistance play a role? Or even sabotage? How can we tell when they have crossed the line from possibly just un-beneficial expectations to harmful or destructive ones?

❖ In *Cinderella*, was Cinderella's meekness really a virtue? Surely Cinderella and her step-sisters would have all been better off if she had left long before the prince rescued her-- Cinderella having relief and her sisters having to face their own selfishness and irresponsibility. Yet there seems to be an element of nobility in her long-suffering. So which attitude is better to maintain?

❖ How is submitting different from being controlled? Are you truly exercising a virtue if you have no real choice but to submit-- if the motivation is fear or obligation and not trust? How can you transform a controlling situation into one where you *can* exercise virtue?

❖ Is submission to an authority strictly physical and willful or must you also conform emotionally, mentally, and/or spiritually? As a commitment to non-resistance (even if only physically), must you then take the arrows shot at you without dodging, deflecting, or counter-attack? Essentially, can you submit externally without conforming internally? Is this right and honest?

❖ How much is submission being supportive and how much is it surrendering? Does it depend on the circumstances? Does it depend on the cost? Where does authority cross the line and become tyranny? Is submission therefore conditional? (Breaking down the word "sub-mission" might help clarify its purpose here.)

❖ If done properly (with willingness and wisdom), how can submission as the differing of your own desires to that of another be a beautiful act of trust or respect? Is it something that is offered periodically or once-and-for-all? Or even in some sense (especially with God), both? Is it something that should be promised?

❖ Ideally, submission is a voluntary (while often continual, not often continuous) yielding of your rights or freedom for the greater good. The exercise of your freedom can interfere with another's faith (1 Corinthians 8:9-13), so the greater good is often to yield that freedom in a given circumstance. List three situations where this might apply in your life: identify someone's struggle, how you might be contributing to it, what freedom you are willing to relinquish, and what greater good you hope to achieve by it.

Integrity

Purity and unity of and across thoughts, acts, and motives

Synonyms: Frankness, Openness, Candor, Good Conscience

Antonyms/obstacles: cheating, deception, deceit, manipulation, duplicity, pretense, fraudulence, rationalizations

Imitation: shamelessness

Hesitations: Exposes your shame; Risk of hurting or offending others; Risk of being dismissed with superficial explanations

Selected Verses

1Sam. 2:3	Prov. 11:3	Matt. 5:8	Titus 2:7-8
1Sam. 16:7	Prov. 11:20	Matt. 12:33-37	Heb. 12:13
1Chron. 29:17	Prov. 13:6	Matt. 15:1-20	James 5:12
Job 2:3	Prov. 17:26	Luke 12:2-3	1Peter 2:16
Ps 25:21	Prov. 24:26	John 15:15	1John 1:7
Ps 41:12	Prov. 29:10	2Cor. 4:2	Jude 16
Prov. 10:9	Jer. 17:9-10	1Tim. 4:12	

Memory Verse

"Search me, O God, and know my heart;
test me and know my anxious thoughts.
See if there is any offensive way in me,
and lead me in the way everlasting."

Psalm 139:23-24

Topic Introduction

Integrity is like a see-through heart: nothing sneaky or hidden. People of integrity are not afraid to look inside themselves and face the ugliness, to question why they do what they do, or to rise up and to do what is consistent with their beliefs even when it seems like such a waste. It means that you refuse to play games with people's minds (including your own) and intend to appear to be exactly who you are. When we practice integrity, we show that God is indeed Ruler of all things, that His promises do work, and that we do not need to be worried about being perfect by our own strength. Like housekeeping your thoughts: if you find something dirty, get it cleaned; if you find something broken, get it fixed; if you find something rancid, throw it out.

What happens to our peace of mind when we do not value integrity?

Literary Examples

Literature
A Diary of a Young Girl, Anne Frank
The Last Battle, C. S. Lewis

Hymn
"Just as I Am", Charlotte Elliott

Short Stories
"Little Red Riding Hood", Grimm brothers
The Tale of the Pie and the Patty-Pan,
Beatrix Potter

Collections

The Moral Compass:
   "The Honest Farmer"
   "The Prayer"

Aesop:
   "The [Donkey] Carrying Salt"
   "The Monkey and the Dolphin"
   "The Thief and the Dog"
   "The Wolf in Sheep's Clothing"

McGuffey's Third Eclectic Reader:
   "Finding the Owner" (36)
   "No Crown for Me" (69)

McGuffey's Fourth Eclectic Reader:
   "Circumstances Alter Cases" (32)
   "The Golden Rule" (51)

Thomas the Tank Engine series:
   "Dirty Work" *(Duck and the Diesel Engine)*
   "The Deputation" *(The Twin Engines)*
   "Hullo Twins!" *(The Twin Engines)*
   "The Missing Coach" *(The Twin Engines)*

Additional Discussion Topics

- ❖ Friendship
- ❖ Fair play
- ❖ Marketing tactics
- ❖ Loopholes
- ❖ Secrets

Activity Idea

- ❖ Mislabel boxes and try to do a task

Topic Analysis

Literary and Dramatic Examples

Cyrano de Bergerac, Edmond Rostand

An Ideal Husband, Oscar Wilde

Idiot, Fyodor Dostoyevsky

"Indian Summer of Dry Valley Johnson", O. Henry

"The Love-Philtre of Ikey Schoenstein", O. Henry

"The Man Higher Up", O. Henry

Mansfield Park, Jane Austen

"Marjorie Daw", Thomas Baily Aldrich

"Schools and Schools", O. Henry

"Shooting an Elephant", George Orwell

Treasure Island, Robert Louis Stevenson

Thought Provokers

- ❖ How is honesty key to integrity, but still distinctly different?
- ❖ Integrity often requires a great deal of vulnerability. How have you seen integrity compromised for the sake of avoiding embarrassment? What positive effects are often noticed when you choose vulnerability instead?
- ❖ Is prayer primarily just keeping an openness with God? Support your argument.
- ❖ Maintaining integrity is a bit like repentance, in that we must search our hearts for the ugliness and acknowledge them to ourselves and to God. But instead of searching for sins; it is a search for hurts, fears, misunderstandings, confusions, doubts, anger, embarrassments, disappointments, brokenness, neediness, blindness, self-blame, shame, and despair. What is a healthy way to deal with them when we find them then?
- ❖ There can be a fine line between being flexible ("wearing different hats") and being artificial ("wearing masks"). Describe the difference. The principles that guide our choices must be consistent-- when no one is watching and when people are watching intently-- even though our choices themselves may not be consistent. Demonstrating integrity in this way is strongly connected to winning genuine respect from others. How is this also closely related to the idea of being free from the tangled web of pretense?

❖ Is leaving a misconception un-clarified always dishonest? What if the other is intent on doing wrong or is incapable of accurately understanding? Similarly, is *creating* an illusion always wrong? What does being "as shrewd as snakes" (Matthew 10:16) mean in light of integrity?

❖ Much of our culture is absorbed in upholding one sort of an image or another. To some degree, we need to be modest and protective of children's innocence and our privacy, but where might it cross the line to becoming a farce? What principle might we apply to avoid becoming more loyal to an unrealistic ideal than to maintaining integrity-- while still preserving a certain degree of modesty?

❖ What sorts of things might we need to sacrifice in order to maintain our integrity? Find three Biblical examples of people who willingly lost something they valued to keep their integrity.

❖ Secret shame is a major obstacle to integrity. From your observations, what are the different ways people deal with the shame they hide inside? How are these all ultimately destructive? What is the Biblical method for dealing with shame? How is this really the only method that truly heals?

❖ Once we develop a strong sense of integrity, it makes so much sense that we might expect everyone else to have it too. Even if a person does not have a strong conscience, we might at least expect the shame of discovery to hinder them from deception. But perhaps surprisingly, it does not. What would be the motivations to scorn integrity? What are the inevitable effects of doing so?

Goodness

Purity and wholeness throughout

Synonyms: Purity, Godliness, Holiness, Righteousness, Blamelessness

Antonyms/obstacles: corruption, debauchery, dissipation, depravity, wickedness, self-righteousness

Imitations: externalism, naivety

Hesitation: Risk in losing your individuality

Selected Verses

Lev. 19:1-2	Ps. 51:10-12	Isa. 57:1-2	Titus 1:15-16
2Sam. 22:27	Ps. 73:1	Matt. 5:6	Titus 2:11-14
Ps. 1	Ps. 112	Matt. 5:48	Heb. 13:16
Ps. 14:2-5	Prov. 2:21-22	Gal. 6:9-10	James 4:17
Ps. 15	Prov. 15:26	Eph. 6:14	1Peter 2:1-3
Ps. 19:9	Prov. 20:9	Phil. 4:8	1Peter 2:15
Ps. 34:19-20	Prov. 28:18	1Tim. 5:22	1John 3:3

Memory Verse

"'But seek first his kingdom and his righteousness,
and all these things will be given to you as well.'"

Matthew 6:33

Topic Introduction

Goodness can be a hard virtue to understand. It is like a good apple-- the inside is sweet and pure (no unexpected worms or bruises) even if the outside is a little lop-sided. Having goodness means that you have worked on keeping the inside clean and orderly instead of just making things look good from the outside. Like an apple, it is what is on the inside that counts-- but often others do not find that out for certain until you are bitten! It means that you are motivated to do what is good according to God's opinion, like a good arrow pointed true to the target. Goodness soaks up the things of God, fights off the bad, and steadily grows. But we cannot even begin to have goodness unless Jesus plants it there first.

What happens to objects that have no goodness in them?

Literary Examples

Literature
Heidi, J. Spyri
Little Lord Fauntleroy, Frances Hodgeson

Short Stories
The Little House, Virginia Lee Burton

Collections

The Moral Compass:
"Appius"
"Brother to the Lepers"
"The Keys of Calais"
"The Line of Golden Light"
"No Greater Love"
"Sheltering Wings"
"True Saintliness"

Aesop:
"The Farmer and the Snake"

McGuffey's Third Eclectic Reader:
"George's Feast" (34)

McGuffey's Fourth Eclectic Reader:
"The Right Way" (50)
"The Best Capital" (87)

McGuffey's Fifth Eclectic Reader:
"What I Live For" (24)

Additional Discussion Topics

❖ Justification versus sanctification
❖ "Working out what God works in."

Topic Analysis

Literary Examples

"A Blackjack Bargainer", O. Henry
"The Griffin and the Minor Canon", Frank Stockton
"The Last Leaf", O. Henry
"A Retrieved Reformation", O. Henry
A Tale of Two Cities, Charles Dickens
The Winter's Tale, William Shakespeare

Thought Provokers

❖ Much like love, holiness is really more of an act of God (1 Thessalonians 5:23-24) than a result from our efforts. Yet we have a crucial part to play in it too. (e.g., 1 Thessalonians 5:3) How would you clarify the difference?

❖ Goodness is a difficult virtue to describe because it seems to require an unconscious application of all virtues. How can we possibly cultivate *that*?

❖ Godliness is not sinless-ness, perfection, or even innocence, but more of a focus on aiming to please God at any cost. So what are some of the common distractions that we encounter? Practically, how can we put on "spiritual blinders" to focus our mental eyes on Jesus better (Hebrews 12:2)?

❖ Righteousness requires effort. If we are not struggling at least a little, then we are going to drift in the opposite direction. Where have you seen this principle illustrated? What are some practical safe-guards we can implement into our lives to keep spurring us on?

❖ Sometimes, especially from a distance, self-righteousness can be mistaken for true righteousness. What are the identifying characteristics of each? And if you suspect self-righteousness, how should you deal with it in yourself? In another?

❖ How far does doing good works generate goodness? How far does goodness generate good works? Why is there so much confusion between them?

❖ A common counterfeit of goodness is externalism (a devotion to outward practices that would appear to purify the inside, but do not) usually manifested in an aloof coolness (which can be mistaken for piety) or an artificial sweetness. Describe each. Are there any other symptoms and how do you recognize them?

❖ Goodness is often proven in the face of confrontation. The good are honestly determined to become right with God rather than to prove to man that they have been right all along-- requiring honest soul-searching. Where have you seen this distinction? And on what grounds is self-justification exempt?

❖ Goodness is frequently tested in small, unexpected ways-- by how we deal with misunderstandings, blunders, errors, mistakes, etc. If we use the situation as a reminder of our own frailty and the vast capability of God, we can persevere better. What are some other common responses to inconveniences and what attitudes do these responses reflect?

❖ Innocence (a beautiful gift itself) is often mistaken for purity, but once innocence is lost, it cannot be restored. How can purity be restored though? What makes the difference?

Chastity[1]

Purity in sensual acts and thoughts

Antonyms/obstacles: lust, sodomy, adultery, fornication

Hesitation: Un-quenched passions

Selected Verses

Gen. 19:1-29	Prov. 6:22-35	Rom. 1:24-28	1Thes. 4:3-8
Lev. 18	Prov. 7:6-27	Rom. 13:13-14	2Tim. 2:22
Deut. 22:13-30	Hosea 1-3	1Cor. 6:9-20	Heb. 12:16
Job 31:1	Matt. 5:27-30	1Cor. 7	Heb. 13:4
Prov. 2:16-19	Matt. 5:31-32	Eph. 5:3-5	1Peter 4:3-6
Prov. 5:3-20	Matt. 19:3-12	Col 3:5	

Memory Verse

"Rather, clothe yourselves with the Lord Jesus Christ,
and do not think about how to gratify
the desires of the sinful nature."

Romans 13:14

---

[1] Please note that this topic is only for the age appropriate.

Topic Analysis

Literary and Dramatic Examples

Anna Karenina, Leo Tolstoy

Carmen, Georges Bizet (an opera)

Jane Eyre, Charlotte Bronte

"The Whirligig of Life", O. Henry

Additional Discussion Topics

- ❖ David and Bathsheba (2 Samuel 11-12)
- ❖ Samson and Delilah (Judges 16)
- ❖ Joseph and Potipher's wife (Genesis 39)

Thought Provokers

- ❖ Write a "Topic Introduction" paragraph describing chastity. (Please use discretion.) What is chastity and why does it matter to God?
- ❖ With chastity, probably more than any other virtue, hard choices need to be made in a moment of quietness-- far outside the heat of the temptation. What specific stances within the issue of chastity do you need to firmly establish in your mind and apply unwaveringly as a set principle?
- ❖ What are some practical "hedging rules" you can make to help protect yourself from even being in a situation where you might either be strongly tempted or pose as a strong temptation to another? Stick to them (even if you become a stickler)!
- ❖ Our body is one boundary that, once it has been compromised, can never be fully regained. How can stoutly maintaining chastity give us a stronger identity, a stronger character, *and* a stronger attraction?
- ❖ Lust is frequently disguised, if only verbally, as love. What are some sure signs that identify lust?
- ❖ Unlike most of the other virtues which have a subtle counterfeit (i.e., diligence/ stubbornness), there does not appear to be any such obstacle for chastity. Is there one? Colossians 2:23 might suggest that there is not. Why might this be? Or if there is, what is it? Explain.
- ❖ Chastity, having more clarity and severity of consequences when violated than other virtues, is really more of a command than a principle. What might be some justifications people would use to compromise chastity of the sake of "something better"? What would be the end result of this?
- ❖ Rahab was a liar and prostitute, and David was a murderer and an adulterer, yet both are highly commended for their faith (though we know David at least suffered dreadfully unpleasant consequences for his sin). What does this tell us?

Overview

"And over all these virtues put on love,
which binds them all together in perfect unity."

Colossians 3:14

Topic Analysis

❖ Many common proverbs and sayings exemplify a virtue. Choose some to categorize. (Beware of "false virtues".)

❖ Literature is ripe with themes of virtue and vice. Identify them in some convenient pieces.

❖ Freedom is a key element in applying virtue. We must choose to be virtuous. At the same time, we are representatives of the Lord. So how far should we act because we *want* to and how far because we *ought* to? (Is driving ourselves by sheer will-power healthy and right? Does it matter how long or how often we employ this? Is relying solely on our desire to act any better?)

❖ Virtues are principles, not rules, and should be applied accordingly. Often it is necessary to apply one virtue over another in certain circumstance, while in others, the other should dominate. But one virtue should only yield to another virtue-- for the greatest good. What happens when a true virtue yields to a false one? (See Appendix A.) Describe some examples you have seen of this as well as the end results.

❖ Is virtue something that we can only determinedly develop? Certainly there are some natural dispositions that lend themselves to one virtue or another. Does this imply that some are born more virtuous than others-- at least in some areas? Or is the fruit of virtue strictly present in those who have been disciplined to apply it by the grace of God?

❖ There are several possible responses to an attack (intentional or unintentional, physical or otherwise). List them. With wisdom, how should we decide which to do? Which virtue do we need to apply most for each of these options?

❖ The four dimensions of humanity-- physical, mental, emotional, and spiritual-- all need to be in good condition for us to be healthy. Virtues are an important way to nurture the spiritual, but there is often a great deal of overlap-- highlighting the inevitable interactions between the four dimensions. Categorize the virtues according to which dimension most completely addresses them. Which group is hardest for you?

❖ Satan is very clever and is determined to distract us on subtle but vital points wherever he can. One of these areas is certainly virtue-- where he blurs the line between what is a virtue and what only appears to be one. While the imitation may not be bad in itself, it can become so when it masquerades as a virtue. Describe the difference between some of the imitations and their genuine counterparts. What are some other imitations not listed? In what ways have you seen them passed off as "goodness"?

❖ As there are so many counterfeit virtues, what makes a virtue? Does it depend on the motivation? Does it depend on the Motivator (Holy Spirit)? Does it depend on the effort? While non-Christians may periodically demonstrate a virtue, can they be considered virtuous? Can anyone?

❖ How many of the virtues are mostly a matter of seeing more from an eternal instead of temporal perspective? While this does not mean we are disconnected from the events of our lives, it does mean that they should not touch our eternal hope (Hebrews 6:19). What are some disciplines that will help us develop this?

❖ Most acts of glorifying God require us to yield our will to Him in some area. Likewise, virtue can be characterized to some extent as a "letting go" of some particular part of ourselves (sometimes only temporarily, sometimes only in a given context, sometimes unconditionally-- but always for a greater good). Reasonably, this process of letting go opens our hearts or minds to receive something else, and hopefully something better. Appendix B lists some possible aspects of this regarding the virtues. Where do you disagree? What might you include instead?

❖ Every good thing-- including virtue-- has a "sting" to it, some very real and often probable threat to our time, comfort, resources, or even well-being. Identifying these particular hesitations can be a solid step to overcoming them. (Yours may be different from mine, so adjust them as necessary.) Which five virtues are most difficult for you and why-- i.e., to what "stings" are you most prone?

❖ The art of applying virtues is something of a balancing act. This is where prayer and the guidance of the Holy Spirit are essential. Identify a problem and opposite views of it, each with a virtuous ground of argument. Or alternatively, write a "There is a time for everything" poem of virtues in the style of Ecclesiastes 3:1-8.

❖ Often in the course of arguments, the goodness of a particular virtue is used as the premise for some action. (e.g., "Patience is a virtue and since you are supposed to be virtuous, you must bear with me.") Even if there might be some truth in the conclusion, this can still be a very difficult dilemma. Give an example of where you have seen this happen. Why is knowing the larger purpose of virtue important? How does understanding the dynamics of virtues often needing to yield to each other help to overcome this fallacy?

❖ "Prayerfulness" is sometimes considered a virtue, for certainly it is a godly discipline we must develop. One might argue that it cannot really be separated from the application of any virtue. Prayer is vital to discernment in most virtuous acts. (How many of the moral dilemma questions can only be answered by praying about the specific situation? What would virtue look like *without* prayer?) But then a similar argument might be made against faith too. Argue for or against prayerfulness as a virtue.

❖ Love is something of the "super-virtue". It acts like glue to hold them all together in proper proportion. It too energizes them all. But it is also mostly an act of God. How does our practicing virtue help to seal this gift more perfectly though? What would love look like *without* virtue? What would virtue look like without love?

References

Aesop's Fables. Kingsport, Tennessee: Grosset and Dunlap, 1947.

Awdry, Christopher. *Really Useful Engines*. New York: Random House, 2001.

Awdry, W. *Thomas the Tank Engine: The Complete Collection*. London: Heinemann, 1996.

Barker, Kenneth L. *Zondervan NIV Study Bible: New International Version*. Fully Rev. ed. Grand Rapids, Mich.: Zondervan, 2002.

Bennett, William J. *The Book of Virtues: A Treasury of Great Moral Stories*. New York: Simon & Schuster, 1993.

Bennett, William J. *The Moral Compass: Stories for a Life's Journey*. New York: Simon & Schuster, 1995.

McGuffey's Third Eclectic Reader. Revised Edition. New York: Wiley, 1920.

McGuffey's Fourth Eclectic Reader. Revised Edition. New York: Wiley, 1920.

McGuffey's Fifth Eclectic Reader. Revised Edition. New York: Wiley, 1920.

The Real Mother Goose. Rand McNally, 1956.

Strong, James. *The New Strong's Exhaustive Concordance of the Bible: With Main Concordance, Appendix to the Main Concordance, Key Verse Comparison Chart, Dictionary of the Hebrew Bible, Dictionary of the Greek Testament*. Nashville: Thomas Nelson, 1984.

"And this is my prayer: that your love may abound more and more in knowledge and depth of insight, so that you may be able to discern what is best and may be pure and blameless until the day of Christ, filled with the of righteousness that comes through Jesus Christ-- to the glory and praise of God."

Philippians 1:9-11

Appendix A: Some Common False Virtues

(While they may be necessary, good, or wise at times, spiritually they are not necessarily so.)

Ambition

Austerity

Beauty

Boldness

Charm

Completeness

Comfort

Composure

Consistency

Convenience

Determination

Diplomacy

Diversity

Economy

Efficiency

Fame

Glory

Healthfulness

Independence

Knowledge

Leadership

Leisure

Orderliness

Pleasure

Popularity

Poverty

Power/Control

Precision

Progress

Propriety

Resourcefulness

Self-confidence

Self-sufficiency

Strength

Success

Tolerance

Tidiness

Tradition

Understanding

Wealth

Appendix B: Virtues as a "Letting Go" of Something

Virtue	What "letting go"	Virtue	What "letting go"
Charity	riches	Joy	inhibitions
Chastity	lusts	Justice	bias
Contentment	desires	Kindness	guard
Courage	safety & comfort	Loyalty	popularity
Diligence	whims	Mercy	standards
Duty	pleasure	Modesty	attention
Earnestness	disconnection	Obedience	understanding
Faith	reason; reserve plans	Patience	time
Faithfulness	opportunities	Peace	worry; disagreements
Forgiveness	blaming & revenge	Perseverance	distractions
Generosity	resources	Repentance	sin
Gentleness	control	Respect	self-preference
Goodness	self-awareness	Responsibility	independence
Gratitude	due	Self-control	urges
Honesty	illusions	Servant-hood	energy
Honor	importance	Submission	rights; own agenda
Hope	future	Thoughtfulness	view point
Hospitality	privacy	Trustworthiness	excitement
Humility	pride	Vigilance	indifference
Integrity	secrets; shame	Wisdom	opinions